FAITH Plus

Building on What You Have Been Given

Michael C. Diotte

FAITH PLUS
Copyright © 2012 by Michael C. Diotte

All rights reserved. Neither this publication nor any part of this publication may be reproduced or transmitted in any form or by any means, electronic or mechanical, including photocopying, recording or any information storage and retrieval system, without permission in writing from the author.

All Scripture quotations, unless otherwise indicated, are taken from the Holy Bible, King James Version, which is in the public domain. • Scripture quotations from The Message. Copyright © by Eugene H. Peterson 1993, 1994, 1995, 1996, 2000, 2001, 2002. Used by permission of NavPress Publishing Group. • Scripture quotations marked (CEV) are from the Contemporary English Version. Copyright © 1991, 1992, 1995 by American Bible Society. Used by permission. • Scripture quotations marked (NIV) are taken from the Holy Bible, New International Version®, NIV®. Copyright © 1973, 1978, 1984 by Biblica, Inc.™ Used by permission of Zondervan. All rights reserved worldwide. • Scripture quotations marked (AMP) are taken from the Amplified® Bible, Copyright © 1954, 1958, 1962, 1964, 1965, 1987 by The Lockman Foundation. Used by permission. • Scripture quotations marked (WYC) are taken from the Wycliffe Bible. Copyright © 2001 by Terence P. Noble. For extensive use. Please email terry@smartt.com for further information.

ISBN:978-1-77069-369-2

Printed in Canada

Word Alive Press
131 Cordite Road, Winnipeg, MB R3W 1S1
www.wordalivepress.ca

Library and Archives Canada Cataloguing in Publication
Diotte, Michael C., 1961-
    Faith plus : building on what you have been given / Michael C. Diotte.
Includes bibliographical references.
ISBN 978-1-77069-369-2
    1. Faith. 2. Trust in God--Christianity. I. Title.

BV4637.D56 2012   234'.23   C2011-906314-X

DEDICATION

This book is dedicated solely to the *ONE*,
Who alone gives us a *Faith Plus* life:

Jesus Christ: my Saviour, my LORD, and my King.
To Him alone be the glory forever.
Amen.

TABLE Of Contents

Preface vii
Introduction xi
1. What Has Been Given? 1
2. First Things First 11
3. Diligence: 15
4. Faith 28
5. Virtue 42
6. Knowledge 51
7. Temperance 60
8. Patience 71
9. Godliness 80
10. Brotherly Kindness 87
11. Charity 98
12. What's in You? 110
13. Making it Sure (Conclusion) 116

PREFACE

Dark have been the days of late. Clouds of uncertainty increasingly loom over every social, economic, political, and spiritual landscape of man's ongoing pilgrimage. Innumerable voices bombard the world scene on an undeniable collision course with one another, scrambling in haste to capture the attention of the unsuspecting souls of men, in hopes of enlisting their attention—even if but for a moment—in the meaningless demands of the day. Lurking in the unpleasant happenings of the current day, yet another frontal assault arises whose chief design is the total annihilation of man and/or any similitude of what he represents.

Man unfortunately remains oblivious to his original purpose or real design. Information long forgotten, given up as but a faint wisp of smoke, yet lingers from a flame long since blown out. Still, above the clamour, a deafening sound can be heard, but not with natural ears… it is not really a "sound" as we would understand it in earthly terms.

Michael C. Diotte

This indistinct cry from the hidden realm reaches to the depths of man's soul. It is indiscernible by man's intelligence, for man has unknowingly forgotten the language he once knew. He no longer recalls the hidden realm along with its customs and meanings. Far too long has he wandered pointlessly in a direction further moved from his destiny and joy. As a result of a choice made long ago, he has become nomadic, forgotten, wasted, driven to self-preservation by any means.

Abruptly, his attention is captivated. Now aware—awake—attentive to something faint, muffled, but nonetheless familiar. The three R's of the human mind scurry to submerge this whisper from the past: reason, rationale, and *raison d'être* move to reinforce the walls of self-containment, the towers of suspicion, and the gates of rejection. The man thinks, *'Tis only folklore—myths and legends passed from sages of a time and an age that surely didn't know any better and was probably the result of someone's strained imagination.* However, the call to his spirit persists. He opens himself to reminisce, to rehearse, and to recall: *That sound?!*

A language—seemingly words—it's a song, moving through the halls of his cobwebbed spirit. Flowing, as it were, like a fresh water stream upon a dry and thirsty land that has not known water for centuries. It's singing—beautifully—a language, yes. But forgotten? No! It is the song of the Ancient One: *Believe! Simply believe!*

This utterance could not be understood by his mind, for his mind has long been unavailable to the words of the fathers before him. He was engaged, occupied with the throes of life here and now. What could be more important? *Believe! Simply believe!* Yes! He remembers—it is the language of faith; the language, culture, and life force of his homeland—a kingdom so magnificent and superb.

Joy floods his being as his parched soul relishes in his newfound stream of hope and the rediscovered path home. He is no longer a pitiful wanderer, having been transformed in that moment into a pilgrim and sojourner—right there, by faith! So it begins—the quest for home—by faith—*plus…*

> *Are you tired? Worn out? Burned out on religion? Come to me. Get away with me and you'll recover your life. I'll show you how to take*

a real rest. Walk with me and work with me—watch how I do it. Learn the unforced rhythms of grace. I won't lay anything heavy or ill-fitting on you. Keep company with me and you'll learn to live freely and lightly. (Matthew 11:28–30, The Message)

INTRODUCTION

Songwriter Reuben Morgan penned the following in his song, entitled "Faith":

> **Verse:** I'm reaching for the prize, I'm giving everything
> I'd give my life for this, it's what I live for
> Nothing will keep me from all that You have for me
> You hold my head up high, I live for You
> Greater is He that's living in me than he that is in the world
> **Chorus:** Faith! I can move the mountain
> I can do all things through Christ, I know
> Faith! Standing and believing
> I can do all things through Christ, who strengthens me[1]

---

[1] Morgan, Reuben. "Faith." Extravagant Worship: The Songs of Reuben Morgan. Hillsong, 2002.

Isn't that the kind of faith we dream of walking in every moment of every day of our earthly lives? Singing about it is not only a good thing, but also inspirational. It enriches the soul with hope that scripture tells us is the capacity, the blueprint, that faith works within (Hebrews 11:1). According to teacher and author Ulf Ekman, "Faith is just a short word, but what it contains is revolutionary."[2]

Throughout this book, I strive to explain faith in Christ, His redemptive work upon Calvary's Cross, and the Word of God. For one to grow in faith, one must feed his or her faith through diligent study, meditation, and confession of the scriptures, for as Romans 10:17 records for us: *"So then faith cometh by hearing, and hearing by the word of God."* Author Beth Jones says of faith, "Faith is one of the most important things for a new believer to understand and develop. To live by faith is simply to take God at His Word."[3]

Notable author and minister Gloria Copeland gives us this reminder about growing in and developing our faith:

> Give your undivided attention to God's Word. Pay heed to what He says. Whatever it says, you believe it and act on it. If you attend to someone, you take care of that person. There is still only one thing that is needful and that is the Word of God. It is the one thing that a believer cannot successfully do without. If you will attend to the Word and spend time in it, every other situation in your life will be taken care of because of the faith, knowledge and wisdom that come from God's Word. Everything we do should revolve around the Word of God because it has the answer to every problem. The Word of God will make your time count. The Word of God will make your life better and your time more productive. You cannot afford to be without the Word.[4]

---

[2] Ekman, Ulf. *Faith that Overcomes the World* (Uppsala, Sweden: Word of Life Publications, 1985), p. 7.
[3] Jones, Beth A. *Getting a Grip on the Basics* (Tulsa, OK: Harrison House, 1994), p. 81.
[4] Copeland, Gloria. *And Jesus Healed Them All* (Fort Worth, TX: Kenneth Copeland Publications, 1981), p. 23.

Introduction

Upon this basis of understanding, we then move on to view and discuss the "PLUS" realm after we come into faith. The "PLUS" is that which scripture clearly reveals in its teaching—as well as through the examples of Christ Himself and His disciples—as being necessary and vital to our growth and maturity. This is how we bring glory to God, easily fulfilling the Great Commission, through consistent and continual growth in the knowledge of Christ, so as to look, behave, think, talk, and walk like Him in the earth. *"…as he is, so are we in this world"* (1 John 4:17).

This book will primarily focus and build its study upon the scripture 2 Peter 1:5–7. We will endeavour to see that God's Word teaches us to add to our faith seven other components necessary to living a full, enriched, and productive Christian life in Christ, as God intended. We will learn that for faith to work to its optimum level, it must have support. Faith was never designed in and of itself to stand alone.

This book is about faith and its associates. Let it be stated here that the faith referred to is a clear-cut, unpretentious faith. A simple faith—not just any kind of faith, such as faith in a human being, faith in a system or in a hero, or even faith in the future. Nor is it about "random" faith or blind faith in the unknown, or even other religions, fabricated thought, or idealistic euphoric realms. It isn't about any of these things. Faith cannot be bought, conjured up, magically imparted, or even found—for faith is not lost. This is about a specific kind of faith—a one-of-a-kind faith, one that transcends and outshines all others. No matter how far, or wide one may search, there is not another like it to be found anywhere, anyplace, or anyhow. It is not discovered or accidentally stumbled upon.

This one-of-a-kind faith can only be *received*, for it is only found in and *given* by One—Him Who is called Christ Jesus! It is called the God-kind of faith. All others are imitations, fakes, artificial, synthetic, and false. This God-kind of faith is available to whoever will come and obtain it. Once received, it will radically change your life, propelling you forward into an adventurous journey that cannot be matched or replicated but only envied. It is not for the feeble, weak, or faint of heart. It is not for the selfish, short-sighted, or self-centered. It is not for

xiii

the greedy, prideful, or charlatan. It is not for those who are living in the throes of this natural mundane life and who are content with such a state. It is for the foolish! The castaway! The hopeless! It is for those who are at the end and know that there is simply no other way but The Way.

It is for the dead: those who have been to the cross of Jesus Christ and died to self. It is for those who see and understand the truth Jesus spoke in John 12:24:

> *Listen carefully: Unless a grain of wheat is buried in the ground, dead to the world, it is never any more than a grain of wheat. But if it is buried, it sprouts and reproduces itself many times over. In the same way, anyone who holds on to life just as it is destroys that life. But if you let it go, reckless in your love, you'll have it forever, real and eternal.* (The Message)

Scripture gives much attention to the God-kind of faith. It begins as a seed (Matthew 17:20) in the reborn human spirit and grows from there to what scripture describes as "little" (Matthew 6:30) and "great" (Luke 7:9). Growing faith from seed to "great" could not be done upon its own but is accomplished through the aid of its associates, whom you will meet in the upcoming pages. For those who are willing, for whoever has come for this one-of-a-kind faith, for those who know that it is only by way of the cross of Jesus Christ—He Who alone is The Way, The Truth, and The Life (John 14:6)—that one comes to salvation, this book is designed for you in a big way!

Jesus states in Mark 4:30–32:

> *Whereunto shall we liken the kingdom of God? or with what comparison shall we compare it? It is like a grain of mustard seed, which, when it is sown in the earth, is less than all the seeds that be in the earth: but when it is sown, it groweth up, and becometh greater than all herbs, and shooteth out great branches; so that the fowls of the air may lodge under the shadow of it.*

Introduction

Bible teacher and author Ulf Ekman says, "The Word of God is called an incorruptible seed (1 Peter 1:23). The Word is like seed or grain that cannot go bad. It is eternal and therefore produces eternal results. In just the same way as a seed produces, the Word will produce in your life."[5]

Your heart is the ground that must be vacant of hardness, cares, shallowness, and offence. The heart's ground must be unoccupied and kept free of such things so that the precious seed (2 Peter 1:1) may be free to take firm root, break forth, and grow into its full potential and design, thereby benefiting all who should come and take refuge in its limbs. Faith is that seed! The realm in which it operates and grows best is known as the "now" realm. So, right *now*, according to 2 Peter 1:5–7, give it some *plus* and you have the God-kind of faith in full expression.

Here's a glimpse of it from God's anointed Word:

And of his fulness have all we received, and grace for grace. (John 1:16)
Which is his body, the fulness of him that filleth all in all. (Ephesians 1:23)
And to know the love of Christ, which passeth knowledge, that ye might be filled with all the fulness of God. (Ephesians 3:19)
Till we all come in the unity of the faith, and of the knowledge of the Son of God, unto a perfect man, unto the measure of the stature of the fulness of Christ. (Ephesians 4:13)

According to Ulf Ekman:

Faith is walking with God, having fellowship with Him and trusting in Him. This is what Adam did prior to the fall. God wants us to have the same level of fellowship and the same comprehension of Him as Adam had. This will make it so much easier for us to release our faith.[6]

---

[5] Ekman, Ulf. *Faith that Overcomes the World* (Uppsala, Sweden: Word of Life Publications, 1985), p. 27.
[6] Ibid., p. 53.

Michael C. Diotte

Welcome to an abundant life of fullness in Christ! It's the life of faith—the life of so much more for every believer. It's the life of Faith... *plus!*

WHAT *Has Been Given?*
chapter one

Paul wrote in Romans 12:3 that everyone who has come to Christ, receiving Him as Saviour and Lord, has received "the measure of faith." The faith we have received is that of Christ's. Galatians 2:20 expounds to us that the life we now live in Christ is by the faith of Jesus. This same God-kind of faith is what we have received at the cross, and it requires us to not only receive it but also add to it—causing faith to increase, be productive, and fulfill its purpose. The diagram below demonstrates for us that the cross of Christ is at the center, or core, of the faith we have received from Him—the God-kind, which is *pistis*.

2 Peter 1:5–8 reveals eight facets mandatory for Christian growth and development. Having these developed and growing in our lives will ensure that we are neither barren nor unfruitful. Eight represents the number for new beginnings, resurrection, or a release from the mundane and earthly. As we grow in our knowledge of Christ by employing these eight aspects Peter speaks about, we most definitely will begin life anew and live in a supernatural way.

Michael C. Diotte

The first of these eight is faith. Much dialogue, writings, and musings are available on this topic alone—however, our purpose is to see the setting or atmosphere in which faith lives, moves, and has its being. We must not only understand how to speak out our faith, or to possess a believing faith, but also grow in our understanding of how real Bible faith actually behaves.

The Greek word for faith is *pistis*, which is the God-kind of faith. Dr. Fredrick Price, founder and pastor of Crenshaw Christian Center in Los Angeles, California, states:

> The God kind of faith says, "I believe it, therefore I WILL see it." The God kind of faith believes first of all, and then confesses with the mouth what it believes.[7]

Pistis seems to have ten basic aspects to it, as discovered in Strong's Analytical Concordance. We will be studying these aspects in this chapter.

---

[7] Price, Dr. Fredrick, *How Faith Works* (Tulsa, OK: Harrison House, 1976), p. 96.

What Has Been Given?

1. Faith
2. Credence
3. Conviction
4. Persuasion
5. Assurance
6. Constancy
7. Reliance
8. Fidelity
9. Belief
10. Believe[8]

Many wonder why their faith isn't working properly. Perhaps it is because our view of faith is often generalized or even superficial.

There is so much more to faith than just reading, memorizing, and confessing scripture. These are, of course, vital to our faith's development, but as we look closer and study deeper about the God-kind of faith, we discover a few things. Generally our faith is probably fine, but specifically, like an automobile needing a tune-up once in a while, we may need to lift up the hood of our faith-mobile and do some fine-tuning so that our faith remains at its peak performance all the time.

Authors James MacDonald and Barb Peil observe that:

> Faith is believing the Word of God. That word "believing" is not "wouldn't it be nice if…" Believing is a lot more than just shallow hope. Believing is, "I've got all my eggs in one basket. I'm in 100 percent." That's faith. But faith is not believing in a vacuum; it's belief based on the Word of God. That's the key."[9]

Upon looking at these ten aspects of *pistis*—the God-kind of faith—I felt prompted to look at it from a mathematical point of view.

---

[8] Strong, James. *Strong's Exhaustive Concordance of the Bible* (Iowa Falls, IA: Riverside Book and Bible House, 1992), p. 58. See #4102.

[9] MacDonald, James & Barb Peil. *Lord, Change My Attitude* (Nashville, TN: Lifeway Press, 2008), p. 147.

3

Michael C. Diotte

For the purpose of our study, faith has ten aspects—or rather, ten sides. In mathematics, a decagon has ten sides to it. See the illustration below.

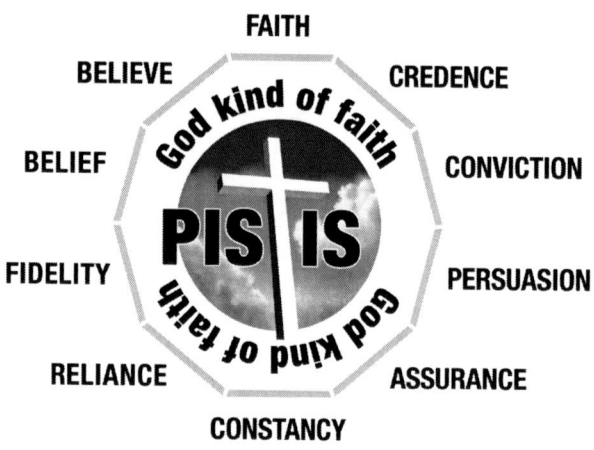

Look at these aspects of faith with an open heart, an alert mind, and keen sight. Never take your faith for granted; it is a precious gift given to us by our Saviour at a tremendous price. If we see any area of our faith that we are weak in or are lacking in, we should rejoice that we have discovered the area of our faith walk that needs attention, tweaking, or a complete overhaul. We must not allow ourselves to become overwhelmed or discouraged, but remain steadfast in tuning up our faith walk. As we do, we will bring our entire Christian life into a newer and fresher season of unspeakable joy and glory.

It may be interesting to note that a polygon (i.e. faith) is a figure whose sides are taken successively, and represent in length and direction several forces (faith's ten components) acting simultaneously upon one point, so that the side necessary to complete the figure represents the resultant of those forces. Wikipedia states, in other words, that a polygon is "an unbounded" (without ends) sequence or circuit of alternating segments (sides) and angles (corners). An ordinary polygon is unbounded because the sequence closes back in itself in a loop or circuit, while an apeirogon (infinite polygon) is unbounded because it goes on forever so that you can never reach any bounding end point.[10]

The faith we received at the cross of Jesus Christ is like a polygon. It is unbounded (without end) consisting of a sequence (succession) or circuit (path) of alternating (interchanging) sides and corners. This is an excellent time to look at the words of Jesus found in Luke 18:27—*"The things which are impossible with men are possible with God."* Jesus gives us a glimpse of God's realm: the realm of faith, where nothing is impossible. Hebrews 11:6 states, *"But without faith, it is impossible to please him, for he who comes to God must believe that he is, and that he is a rewarder of those who diligently seek him."* God's realm is an infinite realm. It is so vast and marvellous that it will take eternity to learn and see everything that He yet has to show us.

Ephesians 3:17–19 reads:

That Christ may dwell in your hearts by faith; that ye, being rooted and grounded in love, may be able to comprehend with all saints what is the breadth, and length, and depth, and height; and to know the love of Christ, which passeth knowledge, that ye might be filled with all the fulness of God.

Here we see faith working with love in the saints to take us beyond the human realm of limitations and stretch us into the vast boundaries (breadth, length, depth, and height) of the fullness of God.

Keep in mind that all the previously mentioned ten aspects of *pistis* work and flow together. One cannot do one without the other. In order for us to move in the God-kind of faith, all these aspects must be operating and harmonizing together. We see in Luke 8:50, and again in Mark 5:36, an example of Jesus demonstrating and revealing how to depart from the fallen realm of man (governed by fear), and walk in the supernatural realm of God (governed by faith and love). Jesus shares the simple secret, which is almost too simple to grasp—Jesus said, "Only believe."

---

[10] Wikipedia. "Polygon." Accessed: April 2009 (http://en.wikipedia.org/wiki/Polygon).

Now let's get started on an amazing journey where success and victory are expected happenings for the children of God, where entrance into such a life of fullness is done by making a simple adjustment to our thinking and actions, forsaking fear and all its associates and coming to the place where Jesus Himself invited us to "only believe."

PISTIS: *The God-kind of faith!*

Earlier we saw that there are ten basic components of the Greek word *pistis*—faith, credence, conviction, persuasion, assurance, constancy, reliance, fidelity, belief, and believe. Now let's take a few moments to define these words, as well as look at a couple of Biblical references concerning their importance in the believer's faith development.

1) Faith: Confidence of trust in Christian theology. The trust in God and His promises, as made through Christ and the scriptures by which humans are justified and saved. Belief not based on what is seen. See Mark 11:22 and Hebrews 11:1, 6.

2) Credence: Belief as to the truth of something. See 1 Timothy 1:15, 3:9.

3) Conviction: A fixed, firm belief, a state of being convinced. See Psalm 119:152 and Hebrews 10:22 (especially in the Amplified Bible). Also see 1 Timothy 6:11, Matthew 9:28–30, and Romans 4:16.

4) Persuasion: A strongly held opinion, a conviction. A body of religious beliefs, a religion, worshipers of various persuasions. A party, faction, or group holding to a particular set of ideas or beliefs. See Romans 4:21 (especially in the NIV), James 2:18, and Galatians 2:20.

5) Assurance: A positive declaration intended to give confidence. A promise or pledge, a guaranty. Freedom from doubt, fullness of confidence, freedom from timidity, boldness, confidence, impudence, presumptuousness. See 1 Timothy 3:13 and Hebrews 10:22 (especially in the NIV) and also Ephesians 3:17, Colossians 2:12, and 1 John 5:4.

6) Constancy: The quality of being unchanging and unwavering, as in purpose, love, loyalty, firmness of mind, and faithfulness. See Ephesians 4:23 (especially in the Amplified Bible), 1 Timothy 6:12, Matthew 9:22, and Romans 4:16–20.
7) Reliance: The act of relying or the state of being reliant. The faith or confidence of trust felt by one who relies; dependence. One relied upon, a mainstay (a pillar, the central cohesive support and stability, the forestay that braces the mainmast of a ship). See Psalm 56:11 and Proverbs 22:19 (especially in the Amplified Bible) and Colossians 1:23, 2:7.
8) Fidelity: The strict observance of promises, duties, loyalty, conjugal faithfulness, and adherence to fact or detail, accuracy, exactness. See Proverbs 16:6 (especially in the Amplified Bible), Acts 6:7, and 1 Corinthians 16:13.
9) Belief: Something believed, an opinion or conviction, confidence in the truth or existence of something not immediately susceptible to rigorous proof, faith. In short, trust. A religious tenet or tenets, a religious creed. The Christian belief. See Hebrews 11:3, 39.
10) Believe: To have confidence in the truth, the existence, or the reliability of something. See John 11:27 and Hebrews 10:22–23, 12:2.

Remember! The God-kind of faith is what you possess right now. The more we study the scriptures and look at our Heavenly Father to see how He uses His faith, the more we'll see how easy it'll be to use ours, for we are made in His image and likeness and we possess the same kind of faith—the faith that overcomes the world and secures victory. It is to this kind of faith (*pistis*) that with all diligence we are to add the next seven facets needed in order for us to properly mature and grow in Christ, being effective, fruitful, and productive Christians for the glory of God. Don't hesitate one more moment; employ all diligence to this wonderful endeavour. The rewards are eternal and everlasting.

Ephesians 5:1 states: *"Watch what God does, and then you do it, like children who learn proper behavior from their parents"* (The Message). Keep in mind that behaviour is learned from others. God's Word is a wonderful wealth of truth and riches available to everyone. The one who remains constant, steadfast, and diligent in the Word of God will be one who enjoys life fulfilled, flourishing and prospering in every area that life extends. God desires that we prosper in every area of our lives spirit, soul, and body (3 John 2). Behaviour is key to our prosperity in all these areas.

We saw previously, in Ephesians 5:1, that our behaviour is to be patterned after God's. He alone is the plumb line for proper behaviour (conduct and mannerisms). Jesus made it so clear for us when He proclaimed in John 14:6, *"I am the way, the truth, and the life."* Jesus reveals it to us—He and He alone is the way (the pattern, conduct, personality, and mannerisms) that we follow after and imitate.

Mark 11:22 states, *"And Jesus answered and said to them, Have ye the faith of God"* (WYC). Jesus gave us this faith at the new birth. The cross of Christ made it possible. It is not our faith alone, for if it was we would have no need for salvation, the cross, or the Christ who went to that cross.

POSSESSORS OF GOD'S FAITH

But now we are possessors of the God-kind of faith. It was given to us freely. It came to us from God Himself. It is He Who has given it to us in a measure. Now we take the measure that was given and use it to imitate Him Who gave it, for He is the designer and Master Architect of faith. He alone knows how and why it works that way. Let us therefore follow (imitate and mimic) and let Him make us into "fishers of men" (Matthew 4:19). God is a God of Faith. Following Him requires faith. Since He knew our human faith was limited, He gave us a measure of His faith when we were born again. His faith DNA came into our dead spirit and we were reborn. We now, like our Heavenly Father, have His faith—His DNA—in our spirit man.

Like children (Ephesians 5:1), we need to study Him, do what He does, say what He says, and act like He acts so that we become like

His Son. Romans 8:29 says, *"For whom he did foreknow, he also did predestinate to be conformed to the image of his Son, that he might be the firstborn among many brethren."* Conformity (correspondence in form and appearance; acting according to God's standards) is not an option; Scripture mandates it.

This is all part and parcel of being part of a family. Children naturally mimic and imitate their parents' behaviour. It is a principle that has existed since the birth of the first child to Adam and Eve. The family of God works the same way. As His children, we naturally desire to copy Him. However, if we are not daily in right relationship with God, something or someone else ultimately influences us and whether we like it or not… our behaviour will begin to be like that which is of the most regular influence (whether positive or negative) in our lives. 1 Peter 1:14–16 says:

> *As obedient children, not fashioning yourselves according to the former lusts in your ignorance: but as he which hath called you is holy, so be ye holy in all manner of conversation; because it is written, Be ye holy; for I am holy.* (Emphasis added)

Family life is a powerful force when operating in its proper design and potential. Today's society is suffering tremendously from decades of family breakdown and family redefinition. Hence, much of the negative and misaligned behaviour that has brought us to such a brink of disillusionment and woe can be sourced back to the family unit suffering from design misuse or abuse.

Being in God's family is a wonderful thing. There is no other experience like it on earth. As in any family, if everyone did their own thing anytime, anywhere to anybody, the family wouldn't survive. The family unit needs structure, guidelines, and principles by which it establishes itself and lives by. Who better to be at the helm of Heaven's family than the loving Heavenly Father, Himself?

As we follow and imitate Him, we will grow to be more and more like Him. As we align ourselves to Him, we will begin to enjoy all the benefits the new birth experience brings, as promised by the scripture. Heaven's atmosphere will pour out over and through our lives into the earth. As His will is in Heaven, so it shall be in the earth (Matthew 6:10). We will begin to see the manifestations that Jesus saw in His life and ministry here on the earth—and more, for we are the global family of God.

Looking at Jesus' life and ministry, we see clearly that He didn't just walk by and talk faith only—He walked in the fullness of grace. He walked in the fullness of life—God's life. He walked in the fullness of the realm that God originally intended for man. He came to give it back to us. John 1:16 states, *"And of his fulness have all we received, and grace for grace."* He came to show us once again how to live, move, and have our being there (Acts 17:28).

There is just so much more for us (Ephesians 3:20). Rick Ciaramitaro, pastor and author, writes:

> Jesus wants you to have an abundant life (John 10:10), but many Christians don't enter into that abundant life. Why not? Because you must go to the cross before the abundant life of Christ can be manifested in you.[11]

Abundant living begins there, at the cross of Christ, springing forth from the seed of faith, which is received from God at the very moment of new birth. The faith seed is not a single dimensional seed, for it comes from God's own faith, life, character, and very breath. The faith we received from Him has more in it than we ever realized.

God never intended for us to only grow in one aspect of the faith He gave; He intended for us to cultivate, develop, and grow in the other seven graces Peter speaks about in 2 Peter 1:5–7. The Christian's walk is, indeed, a walk of faith—but there's so, so, so much more. It's faith, *plus* virtue, knowledge, temperance, patience, godliness, brotherly kindness, and charity.

---

[11] Ciaramitaro, Rick. *Laws of Expansion* (Belleville, ON: Guardian Books, 2001), p. 62.

FIRST *Things First*

chapter two

Growing is a natural part of life. We never stop growing. From the moment we are born again, the scriptures reveal and teach growth in Christ. Growth doesn't come equipped with an on or off switch; it is a natural progression wherever there is life. Growth may be stunted, hindered, redirected, or channelled, but it is growth nonetheless. As believers, we should not only desire to grow in Christ, but expect it. Romans 8:29 reads as follows:

> *For whom he did foreknow, he also did predestinate to be conformed to the image of his Son, that he might be the firstborn among many brethren.*

The Greek word for conformed is *summorphoo*, which speaks of being jointly formed, similar, or fashioned like unto.[12] "Conform" is defined

---

[12] Strong, James. *Strong's Exhaustive Concordance of the Bible* (Iowa Falls, IA: Riverside Book and Bible House, 1992), p. 68. See #4832.

this way: "to act in accordance or harmony; comply; to act in accord with the prevailing standards, attitudes, practices etc., of society or group; to be or become similar in form, nature, or character."[13] God's desire is that we look, behave, think, and speak like His Son—the One Who gave His life for our redemption. The Apostle Peter, knowing this, gives us as believers in Christ the direction in which we are to grow. He lays before us the design or blueprint we must follow and use as our daily guideline.

Success in this area requires conformity, or as we better understood it a moment ago, a modification of our actions and behaviours to the standards, attitudes, and practices of Christ. Since God's desire in the new birth is for us to become similar in form, nature, and character to His Son—as Bob Morehead once stated:

> My face is set, my gait is fast, my goal is Heaven. My road is narrow, my way rough, my Guide reliable, my mission clear. I cannot be bought, compromised, detoured, lured away, turned back, deluded, or delayed. I will not give up, let up, or shut up. I will go on until He comes, and work until He stops me. I am a disciple of Jesus.[14]

BEHAVIOUR UNDERSTOOD

The word behaviour is a noun that refers to the action or reaction of someone or something under specific circumstances or situations. It is the way one behaves, acts, or responds toward others. Behaviour speaks of one's demeanour or manner in which one conducts oneself. It involves and includes body language and facial expressions. According to Wikipedia, behaviour refers to the actions or reactions of an object or organism, usually in relation to the environment. Behaviour can be conscious or unconscious, overt or covert and voluntary or involuntary.[15]

---

[13] Dictionary.com. "Conform." Accessed: April 2009 (http://dictionary.reference.com/browse/conform).

[14] Morehead, Bob. From the tract, "Commitment as a Christian," for Hands of Christ (Roanoke, VA).

[15] Wikipedia. "Behavior." Accessed: April 2009 (http://en.wikipedia.org/wiki/Behavior).

DILIGENCE: *Giving It All*
chapter three

Before we can give the go-ahead to add the "PLUS" onto our faith, the Apostle Peter draws our attention to a very necessary component and mind-set that we must employ to ensure success. He knew and warned the early Christians about false teachers who would come with the intention of hindering or leading them astray, even knocking them off-course (2 Peter 2:1–2). Peter implored them to be attentive to the words of the holy prophets of old and the commandments already given by them, the apostles of the Lord Jesus Christ. He commands them to *"grow in the grace, and in the knowledge of our Lord and Savior Jesus Christ"* (2 Peter 3:18). It is apparent that Peter had growth and development on his heart and mind for the saints of God. Peter was drawing their attention to what it actually means to grow and increase in the knowledge of Jesus Christ our Lord.

Indeed, it begins with faith—the measure we received at the new birth. However exciting and supernatural it is, Peter persuades us to *add* to our faith. In other words, there is faith (conviction and strong assurance)… plus seven more attributes—namely virtue (moral excellence, goodness), knowledge (correct insight), self-control (temperance, self-discipline), perseverance (cheerful endurance, bearing up under trials), godliness (piety, holiness, godly character), brotherly kindness (love toward the brethren), and charity (the God-kind of love which is active goodwill toward others).

It is interesting to note a few things before moving along in our study. First, faith is not the end but the beginning. Like the physical muscles throughout our entire body, faith is the spiritual muscle throughout our new man in Christ. In the body, muscles alone will not bring the body into its full potential. Added to those physical muscles are the vital organs, sinews, and blood. Our spiritual bodies are similar. Like muscles, faith is a powerhouse stored within your new man, ready for growth, for action, for destiny. But faith needs a "PLUS," and Peter knew that, for he openly reveals to us under the unction of the Holy Spirit the marvellous design and wonders of God's handiwork in the new man in Christ.

Next, it is likewise intriguing to notice that the cross upon which Jesus died is shaped like a "PLUS" sign. In 1850, hymn writer Isaac Watts wrote these words to express the truth in Calvary's Cross:

> At the cross, at the cross where I first saw the light
> And the burden of my heart rolled away
> It was there by faith I received my sight
> And now I am happy all the day[17]

For mankind, the cross is where we go to find life—to find the "PLUS" we need to add to that life. The cross is the doorway back to God's realm of life more abundant, life that is to the full, life that is overflowing (John 10:10), and life that is so much more than anything we've ever seen before (Ephesians 3:20). There, where faith is received,

---

[17] Watts, Isaac. "At the Cross," 1850. (Lyrics obtained from www.Higher-Praise.com)

Diligence: Giving It All

darkness is banished and light is manifested. It begins at the cross, and there everything we need to live a fulfilling and enriched life of faith is found. The world would see the cross as a negative—and the cross *is* a negative, to the one without life. However, the power of the cross—the "PLUS" that God provided—will negate sin's effects for whosoever will come to it. Peter intimates that these effects include sinfulness, blindness, barrenness, unfruitfulness, forgetfulness, lack, and being found in a fallen state (2 Peter 1:8–9).

Not only does the cross have the power to subtract from one's life, it alone has the supremacy to add to that same individual's life more than he or she could ever ask imagine or think. Now that's pure mathematics!

The world's thinking is contrary to the kingdom of God, and as a result people continue to this day to live in shallow perception on most everything pertaining to real life. The world seems content to live for the moment: to focus on eating, drinking, and being merry (Matthew 24:38). In such a state was the world found in the days of Noah—and it seemingly isn't much different today. The Apostle Peter expounded on this aspect about the days of Noah in 1 Peter 3:20:

> *Which sometime were disobedient, when once the longsuffering of God waited in the days of Noah, while the ark was a preparing, wherein few, that is, eight souls were saved by water.*

It is worthy of note that Peter should contrast in his writings the state of the world and the need for Christians to grow in the grace of our Lord Jesus Christ and the knowledge of Him by adding to our faith seven other graces. That makes for a total of eight graces that the Christian needs in order to grow in the knowledge of Jesus Christ.

Peter mentions that when Noah and his family were alone on the ark, representing the human race beginning anew, their number totalled eight. Eight is often noted as being the number to represent new beginnings. Noah represented a man of faith acting on God's Word and instruction to build the Ark. His family of seven (his wife, three sons, and their wives) also assisted. Noah needed his family to fulfill the command of God to build, prepare, and launch into a totally new realm of life. Like Noah, our faith needs its family of seven—a wife (charity), three sons (virtue, knowledge, and temperance), and the sons' three wives (patience, godliness, and brotherly kindness)—in order to fulfill the command of God's Word to grow in the knowledge of our Lord Jesus Christ and to be fruitful and abound.

Peter instructs us to abound in these eight graces in order to fulfill God's expectations. Faith alone is not where it's at for the believer who wants to survive in this earth for the glory of God. Too many people settle to simply possess faith and increase their knowledge of faith—how to speak faith and think faith. Far too many believers are settling for sense-faith and have intellectualized their faith in Jesus. Increasing our knowledge of the ins and outs of faith is important and has its place.

Saint, be encouraged: you're on the right track, for this is where all of us must begin. But don't stop or settle there—it is only one-eighth of the equation to living a life that is beyond amazing. Adding the other seven components readies us for an entrance into the everlasting kingdom of our Lord Jesus Christ. This will be ministered to us in abundance.

In Isaiah 28:10–13, we see a principle from God's Word that is often overlooked by so many who scurry about trying to be perfect Christians in performance, as if they are driven by some motivation to impress God through performance or works. (The truth is, God has already been impressed, but not by our performance. He has been impressed by the sacrificial offering of the blood of His Son. He is then pleased by faith and delights in our obedience to His Word.) Here's the principle: *"The word of the Lord was unto them precept upon precept, precept upon precept; line upon line, again line upon line"* (Isaiah 28:13).

We see and learn here the importance of laying a solid foundation both firm and sure in the Word of God. God is not in a hurry to build for the purpose of making a *big* impression for us to be dazzled by. He is, however, eager to build for the purpose of making a *deep* and lasting impression for us to be inspired and changed for His glory. The diagram on the next page illustrates for us that God, Who is a Master Builder (Hebrews 11:10), desires to set each aspect of the eight graces/facets (needed for us to grow fully in the knowledge of Christ) firmly in place in our lives. Each builds upon the other and is kept together by the

Diligence: Giving It All

sacrificial blood of Christ which alone provides righteousness to all who freely receive Him.

Notice, in our illustration, that faith is the foundation upon which all the others are built. Charity (the God-kind of love) is the final. Faith and love set the boundaries and atmosphere for the other six facets to grow and thrive. Faith finds its energy and life by way of love. Galatians 5:6 states that faith *"worketh by love."* We can possess and have *all* faith (2 Corinthians 13:2), but without love the end result is nothing. God is a God of faith, and He is also a God of love.

Our diagram allows a glimpse at the fullness of God's character as revealed in Christ, who is waiting to mature and be revealed in His body, the church. This is how God desires His children to walk in this earth, in His fullness, which John 1:16 says we have received. Ephesians 3:19 expresses God's desire for us to *"know the love of Christ, which passeth knowledge, that ye might be filled with all the fulness of God."* Ephesians 4:13 speaks of our arrival in the unity of our faith and *"of the knowledge of the Son of God, unto a perfect man, unto the measure of the stature of the fulness of Christ."* What an incredible life we have been called to live in Christ!

Faith Plus...!

							CHARITY	1 Corinthians 13:4-8, 13, 14:1
						BROTHERLY KINDNESS	Romans 12:10	Hebrews 13:1
					GODLINESS	1 Timothy 4:7+8	1 Timothy 6:5+11	2 Peter 1:3
				PATIENCE	Hebrews 10:36	Hebrews 12:1	Luke 21:19	Romans 15:5
			TEMPERANCE	Galatians 5:23	Titus 1:8	1 Corinthians 9:25	2 Timothy 1:17	Titus 2:12
		KNOWLEDGE	2 Peter 3:18	Colossians 2:3	Philippians 3:8	2 Corinthians 2:14	2 Corinthians 4:6	2 Corinthians 8:7
	VIRTUE	2 Peter 1:3	Philippians 4:8	1 Peter 2:9	Joshua 6:2	Romans 4:20	Isaiah 30:15	2 Corinthians 12:9
FAITH	Romans 12:3	Galatians 2:20	2 Corinthians 4:13	2 Corinthians 5:7	Romans 10:17	Hebrews 10:36	Colossians 2:7	Hebrews 10:23

Peter shows us the importance of growing in Christ to a richer, fuller, and more personal knowledge of Him. How does one accomplish this? Peter plainly gives us the answer: "Develop the 'Christ-like' attributes." The more we grow in these Christ-like attributes, the more we will come to truly know Jesus and reflect His glory.

One vital key, however, is making sure we are consistently developing a thorough and intimate knowledge of our Lord Jesus Christ. The Greek word for knowledge, used in 2 Peter 1:2–8, is the word *epignosis*, meaning "to become thoroughly acquainted with, to know thoroughly, to know accurately, know well."[18] As we act on the Word of God, using it daily as our guide or map and following its directions, we will begin to demonstrate the Christ-like characteristics, or graces, in our lives.

Now we come to another exciting part of what Peter wrote. Woven in conjunction with each of the eight graces is a small but most important word—"ADD." This may also be understood to mean "supply" (2 Peter 1:5). The word "add" is inferred and also directly involved in bringing each of the eight aspects together in harmony. The Greek word for "add" is *epichoregeo*. In his ministry article, entitled "A Closer Walk with God," Mark A. Copeland summarizes the word as follows: "Originally, to found and support a chorus, to lead a choir, to keep in tune… Then, to supply or provide." This word suggests the idea of "each grace working in harmony with the others to produce an overall effect."[19]

The idea is that each of the eight characteristics is working in harmony with each other to produce an overall effect. Think of a symphony orchestra. Each instrument is added to the other to build the music and bring the score or the notes on the written page to its intended fullness. One by one they join together, submitting their skills, abilities, and potential to the conductor, whose sole purpose is to direct, lead, and

---

[18] Strong, James. *Strong's Exhaustive Concordance of the Bible* (Iowa Falls, IA: Riverside Book and Bible House, 1992), p. 31. See #1922.

[19] Executable Outlines. "A Closer Walk with God: Growing in the Knowledge of Jesus Christ." Accessed: April 2009 (http://executableoutlines.com/pdf/cw_so.pdf).

Diligence: Giving It All

guide them through the musical score as written. The conductor sees the music, beginning to end. Hence, he commands the orchestra's attention, who in turn submits willingly and confidently to him, allowing him to bring it all together, producing music that will captivate, touch, and move the audience, even bringing inspiration and change to the hearts of those enthralled by the living experience.

Peter paints the picture of the eight graces working together in much the same way, each tempered to the other to make the song of life now written in the hearts of every born again believer come alive. As the saint of God yields his or her life to the maestro (the Holy Spirit Who leads, directs, and guides us into all truth, according to John 16:13), that same saint can be assured that the Holy Spirit will bring to pass the fullness of the Living Word within his or her life.

He will temper together in our lives all the eight graces—faith, virtue, knowledge, temperance, patience, godliness, brotherly kindness, and charity—so that the onlookers in this world will be captivated, touched, stirred, and inspired, their very hearts crying out for change. They are awestruck by the living experience of God's genuine love revealed before them in common, everyday folk such as you and me.

The Holy Spirit's goal is to produce the overall effect of touching, inspiring, and changing fallen human hearts, as well as to restore and lift them back up to their original and purposed design. Each trait is necessary, all developing in union with the other. None is to be prioritized over the other or left behind. All must actively play to bring the fullness of the stature of Christ (Ephesians 4:13) to the forefront of every believer's life while on this earth so that the human race everywhere may read the living epistle sent from Heaven upon the hearts of God's own.

DILIGENCE

In a nutshell, the word "diligence," which comes from the Greek word *spoude* (pronounced "spoo-day") means eagerness, earnestness, forwardness, haste.[20] Growth of any kind takes effort, and growing in

---

[20] Strong, James. *Strong's Exhaustive Concordance of the Bible* (Iowa Falls, IA: Riverside Book and Bible House, 1992), p. 66. See #4210.

Christ is no different. Scripture admonishes us to apply ourselves, to be hard working and conscientious where growth in Christ is concerned.

Our development is not to be an accident. If we tend to be casual about our maturing process in Christ, we may find ourselves in a similar situation as the teacher in the following example. In his book, *Folk Songs of Faith*, author Ray Stedman tells the story of a woman who had been a schoolteacher for twenty-five years. When she heard about a job that would mean a promotion, she applied for the position. However, someone who had been teaching for only one year was hired instead. She went to the principal and asked why. The principal responded, "I'm sorry, but you haven't had twenty-five years of experience as you claim; you've had only one year's experience twenty-five times."[21] During that whole time, the teacher had not improved.

The lesson we may glean here is this: We may have been Christians for a number of years, but unless we add to our faith these Christ-like qualities, with all diligence, we are simply repeating the first year over and over again!

DILIGENCE'S REWARD

It's human nature to need motivation. Man needs something set before him to obtain, to reach for and to win. Paul knew this and therefore says in Philippians 3:14–15, *"I press toward the mark for the prize of the high calling of God in Christ Jesus. Let us therefore, as many as be perfect, be thus minded..."*

Peter's writings reveal a reward for those who are diligent in their growth in Christ. He explains that grace and peace are blessings that are available and multiplied to those who grow in the knowledge of Jesus Christ (2 Peter 1:2). Grace represents God's unmerited favour upon an individual, and peace is a result of God's favour upon one's life. Both grace and peace are multiplied (increased and abounded) in the lives of the one consistently growing in the knowledge of Christ.

God's unmerited favour is available to all (Matthew 5:45). However, for those who are "in Christ" and "abide" there (continue, dwell, endure,

---

[21] Stedman, Ray. *Psalms: Folk Songs of Faith* (Mount Hermon, CA: Barbour Publishing, 2006).

Diligence: Giving It All

be present, remain, stand, tarry[22]), as taught in John 15:7, they will enjoy the fullness of God's favour multiplied in their lives through the manifestation of His grace and peace in abundance (Ephesians 1:3, Philippians 4:6–7). God's grace and peace will increase exponentially in our lives through the intimate knowledge of Jesus Christ in our life as we grow to be more like Him. Also included are *"all things that pertain unto life and godliness"* (2 Peter 1:3).

When the scriptures speak of "life" in this framework and understanding, they are speaking of "well-being." As we will soon discover, godliness refers to our conduct being holy, moral, and virtuous, which is a natural outflow of a life devoted to God. God's divine power is available to those who are diligently committed and found in such a state. Further reward and blessing according include the *"exceeding great and precious promises"* of God as well as the high privilege and honour of being *"partakers of the divine nature"* and escaping from *"the corruption that is in the world through lust"* (2 Peter 1:4). All of this and more is available and comes freely to those who are committed to cultivating and developing Christ-like character.

THE REWARD OF NO GROWTH

Whether we want to believe and understand this principle or not, scripture is clear: we reap what we sow (Galatians 6:7). The Apostle Paul also reveals the two realms that we may choose to sow into and reap from—the flesh, or the spirit realm. Each realm produces a harvest (result). The flesh realm pays the dividend of corruption. Corruption literally means "ruin, decay, destroy, and perish."

This sounds like the devil's mission statement from John 10:10, where Jesus reveals Satan's strategy toward mankind: *"The thief cometh not, but for to steal, and to kill, and to destroy..."* The spirit realm, however, pays the dividend of life everlasting. The word "life" in Galatians 6:7 comes from the Greek word *zoe*, meaning the God-kind of life. [23] The word "everlasting" comes from the Greek word *aionios*

---

[22] Strong, James. *Strong's Exhaustive Concordance of the Bible* (Iowa Falls, IA: Riverside Book and Bible House, 1992), p. 47. See #3306.
[23] Ibid., p. 35. See #2222.

(pronounced "ahee-o-nee-os"), which means "perpetual, eternal, and forever."[24]

Scripture teaches that the choice is ours to make (Deuteronomy 30:19). We can choose between two realms—life and death. Based upon these two realms, and seeing what each one produces if we decide to invest our seed there, which would you choose? Ruin, decay, destruction, and days filled with everything that perishes? Or the complete opposite, and so much more than one could ever imagine or think? For that is what the God-kind of life is, and it isn't just for a moment… it is forever!

DILIGENCE AVOIDS

When we make the choice to operate in diligence, scripture teaches that we will avoid becoming blind or forgetful of who we really are as Christians. Author and Christian minister Mark A. Copeland expounds on this by saying, "Our religion is shortsighted if we are not growing in the knowledge of Jesus."[25] When one fails to employ all and due diligence to grow in the knowledge of Jesus Christ, Mr. Copeland says that the saint is suffering from "spiritual myopia and spiritual amnesia."[26]

Our supreme purpose is to become like Christ. In Romans 8:29, the Apostle Paul confirms this:

> *God knew what He was doing from the very beginning. He decided from the outset to shape the lives of those who love him along the same lines as the life of his Son. The Son stands first in the line of humanity he restored. We see the original and intended shape of our lives there in him.* (The Message)

Paul wrote to the Colossians:

---

[24] Ibid., p. 9. See #166.
[25] Executable Outlines. "A Closer Walk with God: Growing in the Knowledge of Jesus Christ." Accessed: February 2009 (http://executableoutlines.com/cw/cw_o7.htm.
[26] Ibid.

Diligence: Giving It All

Lie not one to another, seeing that ye have put off the old man with his deeds; and have put on the new man, which is renewed in knowledge after the image of him that created him: where there is neither Greek nor Jew, circumcision nor uncircumcision, Barbarian, Scythian, bond nor free: but Christ is all, and in all. (Colossians 3:9–11)

Scripture is clear about the focus of the follower of Christ: *Grow* in the knowledge of Jesus Christ. Failure to do so will have adverse effects in the believer's life and reveals that they have forgotten why they were redeemed by the blood of Jesus Christ in the first place. Christ died not only to forgive us our sins; it is so much more than that. He came to set us free from sin, its power and effects, and to redeem us fully back unto God by making us, shaping us, fashioning us, and conforming us to His very own image—never more to be subjugated or dominated by the archenemy of our lives.

Upon the very moment of new birth, the Christian's life purpose and overall destiny is that we become like Jesus Christ! If every Christian grasps this simple truth and pursues it with their entire being, he or she will live a glorious life right here and now upon this earth that will be the envy of every non-believer.

Perhaps the words of the following song, by "Pace Sisters," captures best the desire of the new man in Christ Jesus:

> To be like Jesus, to be like Jesus,
> All I ask is to be like Him,
> Through this hard trial—from Earth to Glory
> Oh, how I long to be like him.[27]

All, however, is not to be drudgery for the believer. Quite the contrary! The life of the Christian is now in Christ, and being in Him is the best place to be, for in Him, the Father of lights, is no variableness,

---

[27] The Anointed Pace Sisters. "To Be Like Jesus." Unsorted. Savoy Records, 1995.

neither shadow of turning (James 1:17). Peter continues to encourage us in his letter, that if we will remain diligent to focus upon making our calling and election sure, we will never fail. *"For if ye do these things, ye shall never fall"* (2 Peter 1:10). He encourages us to work hard, giving it all we have to prove and show that we really are God's people who have been called out and chosen by Him. We see here that being a Christian is definitely not for the lazy or slothful. The one who is committed to doing the work is assured of an abundant entrance *"into the everlasting kingdom of our Lord and Saviour Jesus Christ"* (2 Peter 1:11).

What an amazing promise from the Word of God! If we'll be diligent where our calling and election is concerned (remember, we mentioned earlier about what our supreme purpose is, according to Romans 8:29)—to make them sure, definite, and certain—then we will never fall or "stumble." The Greek word for fall is *patio*, meaning to trip, err, sin, fail, fall, offend, or stumble.[28] Hence, like Jesus Himself, Peter teaches that we are to remain diligent in adding or fully supplying to our faith the seven other graces (aspects), so that we may effectively grow in the knowledge of Jesus Christ our Lord and ultimately prosper abundantly in our walk while here in the earth. As well, we will bring God all glory as a result of a living in the express image and likeness of His Son, our Lord and Saviour—Jesus Christ!

An abundant entrance into the everlasting kingdom of our Lord Jesus Christ is available to all who will be diligent to follow Peter's instructions. We are encouraged not to be lethargic in our walk. God has promised all the redeemed an abundant entrance. He operates abundantly in every area of the believer's life. He willingly gave us His Son. How much more, along with His Son, does he give us all other things (Romans 8:32)?

If we will not only possess, but also diligently cultivate and employ, the eight graces Peter speaks about, we can be assured of living a victorious, triumphant Christian life right now, in this life (2 Corinthians 2:14). We will live jubilant (1 John 5:4), fulfilled lives in Christ, as God

---

[28] Strong, James. *Strong's Exhaustive Concordance of the Bible* (Iowa Falls, IA: Riverside Book and Bible House, 1992), p. 62. See #4417.

has promised in His Word. Brother Mark A. Copeland, whose Bible teaching series on 2 Peter 1 was a tremendous inspiration and influence upon the writing of this book, encourages saints everywhere. He says, "a careful study of these eight 'graces' which lead to 'Developing a Christ-Like Character' is worth the effort!"[29]

Therefore, as we, God's people (those who have been called out of darkness into His marvellous light, according to 1 Peter 2:9), employ every effort we can (spirit, soul, and body)—focusing on Christ our example (Hebrews 12:1–2)—and set our affections to a higher standard (Colossians 3:2), we'll soon discover the true joy of living a life of faith, as intended by God (Colossians 2:6,7)—Faith with a lot of "PLUS."

---

[29] Executable Outlines. "Growing in the Knowledge of Jesus Christ: Developing a Christ-Like Character" Accessed: February 2009 (http://executableoutlines.com/know/know_01.htm)

FAITH

chapter four

In this chapter, we will begin with the first of the eight graces (facets) to our Christian character that Peter mentions in 2 Peter 1:5–7—faith. Peter's motive and goal for writing is to remind God's people about the importance of growing in the knowledge of Christ. To be successful in this endeavour, we saw and learned that we need to employ *all* diligence.

We saw the need to employ diligence in adding, complementing, and harmonizing with our faith seven other graces vital to our mandate to mature and grow in Christ. We will need to work assiduously with resolve to fine tune these eight graces so that they harmonize like a well-trained and well-disciplined symphony orchestra. Employing and working all these eight graces together will create an octave of spiritual harmony that is epitomized in none other than Jesus Christ.

As indicated and implied throughout this book, faith is the principle foundation upon which we must build for our spiritual development.

Faith

Faith is the focal point upon which all the others are then added and harmonized. Scripture is plain and simple in its teaching that to develop a Christ-like character one must begin with and build upon none other than faith!

Let us once again refresh our understanding of the Bible meaning of "faith." Faith comes from the Greek word *pistis*, meaning persuasion, reliance upon, assurance, constancy, belief, believe, and fidelity. Of *pistis*, Greek scholar E.W. Vine says, "Primarily, 'firm persuasion,' a conviction based upon hearing (akin to *peitho*, 'to persuade'), is used in the NT always of 'faith in God or Christ, or things spiritual.'"[30] Bible Scholar Joseph Thayer says of *pistis* that it is "conviction of the truth of anything, belief based upon the New Testament and God."[31]

Faith is a language. It is the language of God's kingdom. For the saint to function properly in their new environment, the language of the kingdom of our Lord and Christ must be learned. There is much confusion, assumption, and wrong behaviour in the body of Christ these days, all because we don't understand the need to learn the language of our new home and kingdom.

The language we were used to speaking in the world as sinners and non-believers doesn't work in God's kingdom. Colossians 1:13 reminds us that Jesus delivered us from Satan's kingdom and at the moment of the new birth translated us into His kingdom. Our citizenship is of Heaven, the Kingdom of God's dear Son, Jesus. Being a citizen of Heaven means we have now been given all the rights and privileges that are afforded all the citizens of Heaven.

We have been legally acknowledged and established as citizens because of our acceptance of Jesus Christ into our hearts and lives, as demonstrated clearly in the message of Calvary's cross. It is important for us to realize that we are not immigrants to Heaven. There are no immigrants or illegal aliens in Heaven. All have been born into the

---

[30] Vine, W.E., Merrill F. Unger, and William White, Jr. Vine's Complete Expository Dictionary of Old and New Testament Words (Nashville, TN: Thomas Nelson, 1996), p. 222.

[31] Thayer, Joseph. *Thayer's Greek-English Lexicon of the New Testament.* (Nashville, TN: Boardman Press, 1977), p. 512.

kingdom (see John 3:3–5 and 2 Corinthians 5:17–21). Anyone trying to find another way or access route into Heaven will be found as a thief and a robber (John 10:1–3). The cross of Jesus is the only doorway into the kingdom of God.

We begin to learn the language of Heaven at the cross. God's grace, revealed in Christ Jesus, is there when we come to Calvary's cross to impart the full benefits of a salvation so rich and free (Ephesians 2:8). It is here, in this wonderful realm of God's grace, that the spirit of faith (Christ's faith imparted—Galatians 2:20) is released to bring us all the way through the transformation process of sinner to saint, of thieves and robbers to citizens of the household of God, of utter and complete poverty spirit, soul, and body to God's salvation (Greek for *soteria*, or *sozo*), literally meaning "rescue or safety, deliver, health, salvation, save and saving."[32] Closer study will reveal that God's salvation is prosperity, wellness, and wholeness for the entire man—spirit, soul, and body.

Now, the task before us is to learn the language of faith so that we may properly function in our new kingdom, and ultimately in our role as ambassadors for Christ (2 Corinthians 5:20). Learning a whole new language and way of speaking, behaving, and thinking can be quite the daunting task. However, we have an advantage in the person of the Holy Spirit (John 14:26, 16:13).

Before we continue, let us define the word "language." According to the Encarta World English Dictionary, the word means:

> the speech of a country, region, or group of people, including its diction, syntax, and grammar; the human use of spoken or written words as a communication system; a system of communication with its own set of conventions or special words; this can be nonverbal as well as employ the use of signs, gestures, or inarticulate sounds to communicate something.[33]

---

[32] Strong, James. *Strong's Exhaustive Concordance of the Bible* (Iowa Falls, IA: Riverside Book and Bible House, 1992), p. 70. See #4991.
[33] Encarta World English Dictionary. "Language." Accessed: March 2009 (http://encarta.msn.com/encnet/features/dictionary/DictionaryResults.aspx?lextype=3&search=language).

Faith

Just as the various languages of the world are vital to the societies and cultures that speak them, so is the language of faith vital to Heaven's society and culture. Heaven doesn't understand the language of the earth, the language of the fallen. Now that we are risen with Christ (Colossians 2:12), it is time to learn a whole new language. This includes learning new vocabulary, grammar, gestures, signs, inarticulate sounds, and nonverbal forms including behaviour, manners, and customs.

For the believer who follows Christ, we have His personal assurance that He will help us. He personally has given us everything we need pertaining to life and godliness (2 Peter 1:3). Paul says we are able to accomplish this because we *"can do all things through Christ which strengthens [us]"* (Philippians 4:13). We need only to study 2 Timothy 2:15 and apply ourselves (1 Thessalonians 4:10–12).

Learning to walk, talk, and live by faith should be the most exciting adventure a Christian ever has. The joy of learning the language of faith is often hindered, and in some cases derailed, because of religion, ideologies, philosophies, and vain imaginations that man refuses to let go of from his fallen life. Anyone trying to carry these into their new life immediately finds internal conflict, a war within the members of their very being (see Romans 7). The Apostle Paul continues in Romans 8 to contrast our new life in the spirit (where the mother tongue is faith) and our old life in the flesh (where the mother tongue is fear).

Perhaps it would also help us to understand faith better if we quickly looked at two key associates in the life of faith: hope and love. Both hope and love remain key to faith's success in our lives while here in the earth. Keep in mind that scripture reveals we are *now* ambassadors for Christ (2 Corinthians 5:20). An ambassador is a diplomatic official of the highest rank sent by his or her representing country as its long-term representative to another. An ambassador is also "somebody who serves…[as an official] representative of something."[34]

By this definition alone, we may glean so much and hopefully begin to better realize our importance in the earth and the current system of

---

[34] Encarta World English Dictionary. "Ambassador." Accessed: March 2009 (http://encarta.msn.com/encnet/features/dictionary/DictionaryResults.aspx?le xtype=3&search=ambassador).

the world as God's people. The church was never meant to be a religious institution, but was sent to be a relational revolution. God wants the world to know that He isn't looking for them to build religion or the institutions that house them. With these, He is unimpressed. Mankind has been trying unsuccessfully to impress God with his own works since Cain, and even more so *en masse* since the tower of Babel.

As ambassadors of the Most High God, it is imperative that we represent Him properly while on assignment on earth. It is vital that we act as He has commissioned and commanded. Habakkuk 2:4 and Hebrews 10:38 remind us how we are to live while on assignment on earth—by faith!

Remember that faith has two key associates—hope and love. As God's high-ranking official, we must be noted as such because of the faith, hope, and love fully operational in our lives and commission on this planet. 1 Corinthians 13:13 says, *"And now abideth faith, hope, charity [love], these three; but the greatest of these is charity."* Notice what Paul reveals and says here! It can have a completely transforming effect in our lives, thinking, and daily behaviour. Paul firstly gives evidence of the relationship that exists between faith, hope, and love. Pay close attention to the truth—these three abide now.

The Greek word for "abideth" is *meno*, meaning to stay, abide, continue, dwell, endure, be present, remain, stand, and tarry.[35] Powerful! Also, Paul says that all three—faith, hope, and love—are abiding (staying, continuing, dwelling, enduring, remaining, are present and standing and tarrying) now… right *now!* This God-designed trio is operating in the here and now. They are here in the present. This is a good thing, as we need them in the present, right now!

We promptly look at Hebrews 11:1 to see the role that hope has in the life of faith: *"Now faith is the substance of things hoped for, the evidence of things not seen."* Hope is the Greek word *elpizo*, meaning to "expect, confide or trust"—which comes from the root word *elpis*, which is "to anticipate, usually with pleasure."[36]

---

[35] Strong, James. *Strong's Exhaustive Concordance of the Bible* (Iowa Falls, IA: Riverside Book and Bible House, 1992), p. 47. See #3306.
[36] Ibid., p. 27. See #1679, 1680.

Faith

In his article entitled "Faith in God," Michael Fackerell, of Christian-Faith.com says about hope:

> Hope is a condition for faith. Hope is "a positive unwavering expectation of good". Hope is for the mind (1 Thessalonians 5:8; Hebrews 6:19), an anchor for the soul. It keeps us in the place where we can believe, but it is not in itself "faith". Yet, without hope there are no "things hoped for", and therefore there cannot be faith."[37]

Thus we see that hope is a vital part of faith, and to its purpose and destiny being successful and fulfilled.

Galatians 5:6 reveals another very important partner of faith. The Apostle Paul writes, *"For in Jesus Christ neither circumcision availeth any thing, nor uncircumcision; but faith which worketh by love."*

In her book *Reduce Me to Love*, author and bible teacher Joyce Meyer comments on Galatians 5:6:

> Galatians 5:6 says faith works (is energized) by love. Knowing the love of God for us as individuals, and learning to allow His love to flow through us to others, is the power behind faith. Our personal love walk gives us confidence before God and enables us to receive from Him what we ask for in prayer (John 13:35).[38]

Love literally energizes and makes faith come alive, giving it the strength and vitality it needs to accomplish what hope is confidently anticipating will come to pass according to the Word of God.

With these two partners—hope and love—energetically involved in faith's work, nothing will be impossible to the one who simply believes (Mark 9:23). Believing is made simple because of the life and energy that hope and love bring to faith's realm. Faith simply and confidently

---

[37] Christian Faith. "Faith in God." Accessed: February 13, 2007 (http://www.christian-faith.com/forjesus/faith-in-god).

[38] Meyer, Joyce. *Reduce Me to Love* (Tulsa, OK: Harrison House, 2000), p. 9.

turns to God's Word and lays hold of what God has already promised. We see this in the life of Abraham, as recorded in Hebrews 11:8–10. Abraham didn't wait to see the end result before he believed and acted. He believed what God told him, and then obeyed and acted on that word. Even though he didn't see physically where he was going at the time, he locked his faith into the Word of God, obeying and acting upon the Word. The result was a life of overwhelming blessing administered to him by the hand of God.

Faith doesn't wait to see it first in the natural realm. Faith draws its confidence and conviction from the Word that comes from God's mouth (Matthew 4:4). It doesn't use the human natural eye to set its standard. Faith uses the eye of the reborn human spirit and, like Abraham, will call those things that are not as though they were (Romans 4:17). Faith calls those things that are in the spirit realm (the realm of God) as though they were in the natural realm (the realm of man). Therefore, faith has confidence and trust in God's Word regarding the things that are promised and unseen.

This confidence and trust is fuelled by a living and intimately close relationship with the Saviour of our soul, Jesus, and a deep communion with the One He sent to comfort, lead, and guide us into all truth—the Holy Spirit. A vibrant, living faith comes out of a vibrant living relationship with Jesus Christ. Too many people still misunderstand that in order for faith to successfully work and rise to its full *dunamis* ability (miracle-working power), as revealed in the scriptures, it must be in a daily active relationship with hope and love. Without this, faith is dry, brittle, and dead.

Throughout scripture, relationship is both taught and implied with God and His Word. God did not come to set up a religious institution, but a relationship revolution. The Word of God is about relationship lost and restored. Man, however, has built the Word around his fallen state and institutionalized it into a variety of religions, just to appease his own fallen and guilty conscience.

Adam lost his standing before God because of broken relationship. This happened because of sin (rebellion, disobedience, and pride). The cross represents relationship restored. Mankind faces a choice: it can be institutionalized or revolutionalized. One leads to religion, with all of its pomp, rules, and legalisms, while the other leads to relationship, with all the fullness of life and true freedom that anyone could ever imagine, ask, or think. The cross is the way back into a relationship with the Most High God. No one who truly enters it with full and complete surrender have ever regretted doing so. The journey into such a relationship is done simply by placing faith in God's Word (Jesus Christ), whose life and energy come from hope and love.

John 15:7 reveals the key to such a vibrant relationship: *"If ye abide in me, and my words abide in you, ye shall ask what ye will, and it shall be done unto you."* Abiding is the key to having what you ask for come to pass, according to the Word of God. When we abide in the Word and God's Word abides in us, we are living a life that is completely governed by the realm of God's Word. It isn't about the do's and do not's, important though they may be. Faith has a legal side whereby it operates by principles, guidelines, and standards that God has set forth in His Word.

But faith also has a vital side, a side so many miss completely or just plain do not understand. The vital side is the side that adds character, behaviour, attitudes, as well as the daily thinking and sayings of faith. It's about relationship. Faith has a relationship with God's Word that is real and alive. Faith feeds and draws its very life from the Word of God. To abide in the realm of God's Word is to take up residence in His Word. Faith also infers letting the Word take residence in every aspect of our lives, thoughts, speech, and behaviour—to be influenced and governed by the Word (which Romans 10:8 says is the "word of faith"). The goal before us is to look and act like Jesus, to be conformed to His image and likeness so that people know we belong to Him.

Too many people have wrongly concluded that faith is blind—trusting for no good reason. Unfortunately, there are many teaching on the subject of faith who simply do not understand it. Bible faith is not belief in something without evidence. Quite the contrary! Bible faith needs evidence in order to operate and function correctly and efficiently, as we have previously seen in Hebrews 11:1. Bible faith is a trust and confidence based upon strong evidence.

Michael C. Diotte

Pastor Ulf Ekman, founder and director of Word of Life Church in Uppsala, Sweden, pens the following in his book, *Faith that Overcomes the World*, in relation to Hebrews 11:1:

> Faith is not a loose assumption or something about which we are not sure. Faith is a substance and an evidence. Faith is not having a generally optimistic attitude about something you are hoping will work out. Faith is a conviction. It is something about which you are fully convinced and from which you cannot be moved, no matter how things around you may appear. Your circumstances may be completely contradictory, but faith is the evidence of things not seen—this kind of faith produces supernatural results. This is the kind of faith that does *not* shrink back from insurmountable odds but sees what God can do instead. It is convinced about things which cannot be seen and even causes great mountains to move. Jesus calls this "faith of the heart", a faith which produces results.[39]

Faith is fundamental to our relationship with God. Without faith, we would not be able to please God (Hebrews 11:6). Faith is the force that governs or holds together the realm of God. It is the language of the spirit realm of God, and it is also the creative force of God Himself that brought everything into existence. All that exists was and is made by Him and for His glory (John 1:3).

FAITH REQUIREMENTS

Faith is the very groundwork for our relationship with God. As mentioned already, faith is required to please God. Hebrews 11:6 announces, *"But without faith it is impossible to please him: for he that cometh to God must believe that he is, and that he is a rewarder of them that diligently seek him."* The writer of Hebrews reminds us that we must believe (have faith, confidence, and trust) that He is. For the one who

---

[39] Ekman, Ulf. *Faith the Overcomes the World* (Uppsala, Sweden: Word of Life Publications, 1989), pp. 8–9.

draws back, as indicated by Hebrews 10:35–39, God has and finds no pleasure in.

There are actually two realms at work. Man must decide which one he will operate within. This choice is not to be treated as a shopping excursion or "which restaurant shall we eat at?" type of thing; this choice is made from the thought of literally moving from one place to another in order to take up permanent residence. These realms are "faith" and "fear," or "possible" and "impossible."

So we understand that faith is what pleases God, and it must believe that God is. Faith is the core factor and building block in our salvation and ministry to God. John 1:12 underlines faith as being the key that opens the door to salvation. It is the propelling force in our life of service to God (Galatians 2:20). One who has no faith cannot begin a relationship with God, for He is not pleased with anything else but faith.

Faith is not only our foundation to maturity in Christ; it is a power source on-hand for all who believe (Ephesians 1:18–20). It is the vehicle and means for God's power to flow into the lives of His people. The Apostle Paul describes it as potential and ability beyond our imagination (Ephesians 3:20–22). John expresses that faith enables us to overcome (1 John 5:4–5). We find in Paul's letter to Timothy that we need to call it to our remembrance and keep ourselves stirred up (2 Timothy 1:5–6), making full proof of our ministry (2 Timothy 4:5)—watching, enduring, and working.

To grow in our knowledge of Jesus Christ, we need power from God. He has given us faith as our power source. Peter made no mistake in first bringing our attention to faith as being the first and primary stone to lay down in our growth in the knowledge of Christ. Faith is the base foundation upon which God's people are to build a close relationship with Him. Without this primary and vital building stone in place, we are certain to build lives that are haphazard, weak, and full of fear, anxiety, worries, and doubts. Satan will make sure to torment the believer whose life is not built according to scriptural principles, as found in Colossians 2:7—*"Rooted and built up in him, and stablished in the faith, as ye have been taught, abounding therein with thanksgiving."*

Understanding what we have just learned, let us pause briefly to pull into our awareness a few other factors about our faith. Once faith is received at the new birth experience, it needs to develop and mature. Faith is based solely upon the Word of God. Its development and growth are directly linked to one source alone—God's Word. Romans 10:17 explains this in terms for all to grasp: *"faith cometh by hearing, and hearing by the word of God."* John 20:31 reinforces what we just heard from Romans, telling it this way: *"But these are written, that ye might believe that Jesus is the Christ, the Son of God; and that believing ye might have life through his name."* As faith grows, keep in mind that it does not draw its identity from the world system, nor does it seek to behave and model itself from the same. Faith does not attend the school system of the world of the fallen man. Rather, it puts its entire focus and attention upon God and Jesus Christ, its Author and Finisher (Hebrews 12:2).

Faith rivets its eyes to Christ and the Word of God; this is how we are then able to *"walk by faith, not by sight"* (2 Corinthians 5:7). Faith unrestricted by man's personal fears and hang-ups will diligently read and study the Word of God (2 Timothy 2:15, Joshua 1:8). Remember that faith feeds on God's faithfulness (His Word). Fear (faith's archenemy) feeds on Satan's pride, rebellion, and suspicion.

Before we can put the "PLUS" with our faith, let us do a bit of housekeeping where our faith is concerned—or perhaps we may coin the term "faith-keeping." We should keep the following in mind regarding our faith's development in Christ:

1) Hebrews 3:12–14 teaches us to guard against unbelief.
2) Follow Paul's directive, as given in 1 Timothy 6:9–12, to flee materialism (undue concern for the things of this world), pursue faith (by feeding continually on the Word), and fight the good fight of faith (be active in propagating the faith—Jude 3).

FAITH'S DEMONSTRATION

As we now begin to add to our faith the "PLUS" aspect of what Peter teaches in scripture (2 Peter 1:5–7), we once again draw into our faith's development the aspect of behaviour. As faith grows and draws

Faith

from the Word of God, it will begin to act, behave, and demonstrate itself like Jesus did while He was here on the earth.

It is important for the Christian to know that faith loves to obey the Word of God. Because faith draws its very life essence from the Word of God, it has no problem following and obeying the Word. The easiest thing for faith to do is obey the Word. Now, many may find that to be a difficult thought to ingest, but that it is the truth. What we need to understand is the reason why we struggle or fail to obtain results with our faith; it is not because faith doesn't want to succeed or that our faith isn't enough, for even Jesus reminds us in His gospel teachings that if we had faith the size of a mustard seed we could say to this mountain be removed and it would be removed (Matthew 17:20). So size is not the problem. The problem is the other forces or issues that we allow into our heart, which hinder our faith from achieving its full potential.

Consider this: the Bible teaches us that the friends and associates that are good for faith to hang out with, so that it may maximize its full potential, are hope and love. If the forces of hope and love are not allowed into and cultivated in our hearts, faith will have a difficult time producing. If we fill our hearts with other forces from this world's system, Satan's kingdom of darkness, or our own religious and fallen mindsets, our faith will struggle to survive. The parable of the Sower Sowing the Word, as found in Mark 4, expounds this principle of man's heart and the different atmospheres that faith finds itself in, and the corresponding results.

In a nutshell, faith loves the Word and loves to obey and act on it. It is the nature of faith to do so. The Word's expectation is total obedience from the point of salvation onward (Hebrews 5:9). One obeys the Word by obeying the commands of the gospel of Christ. The Word of God command us to

1) Believe in Him (Mark 16:15–16).
2) Repent of sins (Acts 2:38, 17:30).
3) Confess Jesus (Matthew 10:32, Romans 10:9–10).
4) Be baptized for the remission of sins (Acts 2:38, 22:16).

We demonstrate our faith for others to see by obeying from the heart the teachings openly revealed in the Word of God (Romans 6:17).

Michael C. Diotte

Faith demonstrates itself to others daily by living for Jesus. This is done by simply trusting, acting upon, and doing the words Jesus spoke. Matthew 6:33 instructs us to *"seek ye first the kingdom of God, and his righteousness."* Luke 6:46 says, *"And why call ye me, Lord, Lord, and do not the things which I say?"* And according to Matthew 28:20, *"Teaching them to observe all things whatsoever I have commanded you: and, lo, I am with you always, even unto the end of the world."*

Faith demonstrates itself through obedient behaviour, but also by trusting. It confidently relies upon the Words of Jesus.

> *Let not your heart be troubled: ye believe in God, believe also in me. In my Father's house are many mansions: if it were not so, I would have told you. I go to prepare a place for you.* (John 14:1–2)

Faith merely believes wholeheartedly what Jesus promises. As we understand how and why faith grows, maturing the way it does, we'll see that it is a normal response and behaviour to the love and hope of God at work in our lives. We'll then begin to reject all negative patterns and behaviours, clearing a better path for our faith to grow into the vibrant, fully alive, spiritual force God intended.

We must, however, choose to follow Christ (Matthew 4:19), allowing and trusting Him to make us into all that He has promised: sons and daughters of the Most High God, ambassadors of the living and victorious Christ, and as Peter puts it in 1 Peter 2:9, *"But ye are a chosen generation, a royal priesthood, an holy nation, a peculiar people; that ye should shew forth the praises of him who hath called you out of darkness into his marvellous light."* That is how God sees and desires each of you to be. Your faith knows this and, from the moment it began in your spirit at the new birth, has already begun to head in this direction. Be determined today to release your faith to pursue its destiny and intended course as mapped out in the Word of God. Make a quality decision to be an example of one who walks by faith in Jesus and is totally dependent and yielded to God, His Word, and His destiny for your life—not one who walks by the sight of their natural eyes or what they can accomplish in their own strength.

Now that you have that settled, welcome to the realm of God's Word, where nothing is impossible—only believe! From here on in, it is faith… PLUS—the realm of so much more than ever before.

VIRTUE: *Striving For Excellence*
chapter five

Developing a Christ-like character is a necessity to grow in the knowledge of Jesus Christ. In his letter to the churches, Peter teaches this importance, coupling with it the mandate that every believer add to their faith. Peter expounds on eight graces necessary for proper maturity in Christ, as found in 2 Peter 1:5–7.

We learned that all eight work in conjunction with each other and that, as God's people, it is expected for us to employ *all* diligence so that we may abound in them. It may be an excellent opportunity to remind ourselves again that the number eight is the number for new beginnings. This is a great source of encouragement and an excellent blueprint for the saint of God to keep before their eyes. As we give all diligence to grow in Christ, we will come into the full stature of Christ—into a new beginning, readied for the supernatural happenings of God.

It all begins and ends with and in Christ! He is the Alpha and Omega, the beginning and end (Revelation 21:6). Ephesians 2:20 teaches that

Virtue: Striving For Excellence

we, His people, also known as the household of God, are *"built upon the foundation of the apostles and prophets, Jesus Christ himself being the chief corner stone."* It starts and ends with Jesus.

We are being built, shaped, fashioned, and formed to look, think, speak, and behave like the firstborn (Romans 8:29). It is, as some have said, a spiritual construction project. With Christ as the chief cornerstone—the apostles and prophets being the foundation—our part now begins with faith. Faith is what pleases God (Hebrews 11:6) and is the catalyst for walking in God's realm of possibilities (Mark 9:23).

Growing and becoming like Christ does not happen by faith alone. Peter reminds us that faith requires a commitment from our lives—diligence, and not just a little, but *all*. Without hesitation, we better understand faith and have committed to laying this stone of faith upon the foundation (apostles and prophets) and chief cornerstone (Jesus Christ). We are equipped, geared up, and all set to lay the next stone in conjunction with what is already laid in our new life in Christ.

The Apostle Peter moves our attention for growth in the knowledge of Christ Jesus immediately over to virtue. He tells us to add virtue to our faith. Faith is not to stand alone, and although it is a rudimentary, vital strength in our growth process, there is more to come. When Peter speaks of adding, he speaks of putting something into or joining something together with another. It is like adding an ingredient to a cake mix, for it is part of the recipe's requirements. To add is to increase the effect of something—to enhance, augment, and complement it.

The Greek word for "add" is *epichoregeo*,[40] indicating that these two must now work together like a musical symphony; each instrument has its part to play and contributes to the overall musical orchestration. Thus, in order to grow further upon our foundation of faith in Christ, scripture requires us to add the attribute of virtue.

VIRTUE CLARIFIED

The term "virtue" is infrequently used in the New Testament. This, however, does not minimize its importance, for Peter moves virtue next

---

[40] Strong, James. *Strong's Exhaustive Concordance of the Bible* (Iowa Falls, IA: Riverside Book and Bible House, 1992), p. 32. See #2023.

in line to faith. In Philippians 4:8, Paul uses the term once: *"If there be any virtue, and if there be any praise, think on these things."* Peter uses it four times in his letters, two of those times being found within the context of our study.

1) In 1 Peter 2:9—*"...proclaim the praises (virtue) of him"* (NKJV)
2) In 2 Peter 1:3—*"...that hath called us to glory and virtue."*
3) Twice in 2 Peter 1:5—*"And beside this, giving all diligence, add to your faith virtue; and to virtue knowledge."*

The NIV Bible translates the word virtue as "goodness." The NASB uses the term "moral excellence." Wycliffe renders it as "excellence," whereas JFB explains it as "manly excellence." Clarke and Barnes employ the terms "courage, fortitude, vigour, and energy." The Message Bible uses the terminology "good character."

The Greek word for "virtue" is *arete*,[41] meaning manliness (valour), excellence, and praise. New Testament Greek Scholar A.T. Robertson, a professor for Southern Baptist Theological Seminary at Louisville, Kentucky and also author and lecturer, said of the word "virtue" that it is an "old word for any preeminence (moral, intellectual, military)."[42] Robertson stated that the Greeks themselves used the word to describe "any mental excellence or moral quality or physical power." The word was also used to represent a concept of excellence in all phases of life, to which the Greeks strove to attain (mentally, morally, and physically).

Peter wisely brings virtue next to faith, for virtue is that godly trait which has the desire to excel and be strong in every area and venture undertaken. Virtue is the determined and motivated characteristic that presses forward for excellence in our heart-faith relationship with Jesus Christ. Virtue adds itself to our faith so that our faith may strive for excellence in all of its pursuits in Christ.

The Free On-Line Dictionary by Farlex says virtue is Latin for "manliness." It continues by stating that in philosophy it is the quality

---

[41] Ibid., p. 15. See #703.
[42] Christian Classics Ethereal Library. "Biography of A.T. Robertson." Accessed: March 2009 (http://www.ccel.org/r/robertson_at).

Virtue: Striving For Excellence

of good in human conduct.[43] It becomes clearer that the common thought behind virtue is strength, valour, and moral excellence. Virtue works together on a continual basis with faith. Virtue strengthens faith's ability to reach and press forward for the high calling of God in Christ Jesus (Philippians 3:14). Without virtue, faith will struggle in its efforts to obtain the prize. Faith then is left open as prey to its enemies, perhaps even finding itself shipwrecked (1 Timothy 1:19). God designed faith to have partnerships and relationships. It must not work alone to fulfill its God-given purpose and design. If faith cannot work, it will die. James 2:26 enlightens us by saying, *"So faith without works is dead also."*

Virtue arrives to add itself, its strength, manliness, valour, excellence, and praise to faith's pursuits. Joined together, the desire for excellence in service to our God increases and comes alive. Faith becomes dynamic, manly, and most excellent, rising to give praise and glory to God. The believer begins to look and act more like Christ. The Christ-like one now begins to operate in a faith that is not harsh, rigid, religious, and binding. His diligence to increase rewards him with a tremendous position of victory, along with all of its recompense and blessings. Virtue puts added "PLUS" into the believer's faith life and walk. Thus, they begin to abound more and more.

In this lifetime, the view of becoming like Christ and being holy as he is holy (1 Peter 1:15–16) is now clearer. Faith becomes enthusiastic and energetic as it pursues its goal to be like the Master. For it is Jesus Who taught His disciples to go all-out for excellence, as Matthew 5:48 indicates. He died to make this pursuit possible for His followers (Hebrews 10:12–14). He then gave gifts to guarantee our becoming like Him in virtue, manliness, excellence, and praise (Ephesians 4:11–13).

The Apostle Paul encourages virtue (excellence) in the disciples as an aim and purpose in his ministry (Colossians 1:28–29). He instructed the Corinthians to this end in 2 Corinthians 7:1. Paul wrote to Timothy, his own son in the faith:

---

[43] The Free Dictionary. "Moral Excellence." Accessed: March 2009 (encyclopedia2.thefreedictionary.com/moral+excellence).

Michael C. Diotte

> *All scripture is given by inspiration of God, and is profitable for doctrine, for reproof, for correction, for instruction in righteousness: that the man of God may be perfect, thoroughly furnished unto all good works.* (2 Timothy 3:16–17)

The Christian who follows Peter's instructions along with his map to growing in the knowledge of Christ soon discovers the joy of what it is truly like to be like Christ. Similar to building a home, a wall, or putting together a puzzle piece by piece, as each step is taken, or each piece put into its place, the figure begins to take shape and become more apparent.

Virtue adds a quality, a dimension, to one's faith that thrusts them deeper in their relationship with Christ. Faith is no longer weighty, legalistic, flimsy, or dead. It is fresh, alive, invigorated, and readied for the challenges ahead—firm, resolute, and unwavering in its focus to fulfill the Master's commission to "Go" (Matthew 28:19–20, Mark 16:15–20). Peter prayed for grace and peace to be multiplied to them (2 Peter 1:2), and then goes on to exhort that they press on to grow and obtain more.

Commenting upon this passage of scripture found in 2 Peter 1:5–7, Biblical Exegete and pastor Matthew Henry says:

> We should, as we have opportunity, exhort those we pray for, and excite them to the use of all proper means to obtain what we desire God to bestow upon them; and those who will make any progress in religion must be very diligent and industrious in their endeavours.[44]

Henry further comments on Peter's direction on growing in the knowledge of Christ by stating, "Here we cannot but observe how the believer's way is marked out step by step."[45] He also reminds us to follow the markers Peter so meticulously put before us, and also to take every opportunity to encourage each other to continue on such a wondrous way.

---

[44] Henry, Matthew. *Matthew Henry's Commentary on the Whole Bible* (Peabody, MA: Hendrickson Publishers, 1999), p. 2434.
[45] Ibid.

Virtue: Striving For Excellence

Faith and virtue working in partnership set the tone for an amazing pilgrim adventure. So let's consider at this time the importance of the Word of God in developing the quality of virtue in our lives so that our faith may benefit completely and abundantly, so that we lack nothing.

DEVELOPMENT OF VIRTUE

Previously we found in 2 Timothy 3:16–17 the objective of God's Word. Let's review the scripture again:

All scripture is given by inspiration of God, and is profitable for doctrine, for reproof, for correction, for instruction in righteousness: that the man of God may be perfect, thoroughly furnished unto all good works. (2 Timothy 3:16–17)

God's Word is designed to make us perfect, mature, complete, lacking nothing. Our role, therefore, with regards to the Word is to give ourselves to reading and meditation upon the Word. As we do, the Word of God promises the ensuing benefits:

1) Psalm 1:1–3—we shall be like a strong and fruitful tree.
2) Psalm 119:97–99—we shall grow in wisdom and understanding.

God calls us to a fruitful, bountiful, and abundant life that began the moment we came to the cross of Christ. Paul exhorts us to therefore meditate upon those things that contain virtue (Philippians 4:8).

Scripture is teeming with men and women whose lives reflect the graces Peter teaches in 2 Peter 1:5–7. If we'll study and glean from their lives those qualities, employing them with all diligence in our lives, we will then wisely build upon their testimonies and steer clear of the many snares, traps, and wiles Satan surely has laid out for the unsuspecting saint.

Paul persuades us to emulate those things in his life that line up with the Word of God (Philippians 4:9). He is transparent about his own desire and persistent pursuit of virtue (manliness, valour, excellence, praise) in Philippians 3:12–14. He calls to our attention the need to focus and press forward. He didn't consider himself to have already reached and apprehended; rather, he reveals that he kept himself stirred up and focused on the quest of Christ Jesus. There's always room to grow. Therefore, turn from what's behind, forget about it, move on, and snap to it. There isn't time to waste.

In the commentary of the Life Application Bible, we find the following words written regarding Paul's mandate in Philippians 3:12–14:

> Paul said his goal was to know Christ, to be like Christ, and to be all Christ has in mind for him. This goal absorbed all his energy. This is an example for us. We should not let anything take our eyes off our goal—Christ. With the single-mindedness of an athlete in training, we must lay aside everything harmful and forsake anything that may distract us from being effective Christians.[46]

In simple terms, Paul seeks to persuade us by these points:
1) Never rest on your past successes.
2) Never allow past mistakes or failures to hinder you, even for a moment, from moving forward to victory.
3) Reach and keep on reaching forward to what is yet in Christ.
4) Be optimistic, drawing strength, encouragement, and vision from the Word of God. Don't be a pessimist—it is a great enemy of your faith and will constantly sabotage your victory. Besides, "pessimist" is just another way of saying "pest-I-missed." Pests have a way of bugging both you and your faith, so pull out the flyswatter (Word), permanently putting it out of its misery. Then, move along in the joy of the Lord to the victory prepared for you.
5) Fix your eyes on the prize prepared for you in Christ and press on (2 Timothy 4:8, 18). Virtue is the manly quality of excellence and valour that just doesn't quit or give up.

---

[46] Life Application Bible (Wheaton, IL: Tyndale House Publishers, 1989), p. 2090.

Virtue: Striving For Excellence

In Dallas, during a Sunday morning service in 2003, Bishop T.D. Jakes declared, "Never, never, never give up!" If we will allow virtue to grow and develop in our lives—to work in harmony with our faith—then virtue will demonstrate that same attitude and come alongside your faith, exhorting it to "never, never, never give up!" Thus Paul, like Bishop Jakes, urges and presses the Christian to develop and possess this same mindset. In doing so, virtue will add to your faith resilience, buoyancy, and hardiness, thereby enabling it to endure the throes which life all too often presents.

The Apostle Paul, a man of virtue, wrote to Timothy, his son in the faith, reminding him to place top priority upon the Word of God (1 Timothy 4:13–16). Paul draws to Timothy's attention the importance of others seeing the results of God's Word at work in and through our lives. Allowing virtue to actively work in your life alongside your faith will cause your faith to shine brightly for others to see. Christians are a reflection of Christ and show the world a picture of what heaven is truly like. Think on it for a few moments. Every time anybody looks at you, they are catching a glimpse of what heaven is like. Based upon what they see, would they want to go there?

So let us give attention to Paul's words and shore up the loose areas in our lives by committing anew to:
1) Excel in our relationship with God.
2) Read His Word daily and spend time listening to Him.
3) Pray (communicate) without ceasing.
4) Excel in service to God.
5) Develop our talents and gifts for God's glory.
6) Be a blessing to others using the talents and abilities God gave us to benefit and prosper His body.

Employing virtue in our faith life will cause us to flow well with others and be a fine example of Christ. People will see the progress of faith in our lives. God will then be glorified.

Virtue will not allow faith to hide and be uninvolved. Manly and excellent in its ways, virtue wants to bring the believer's faith into active service in the local church assembly. That's where the body of Christ is, so it must also be there to encourage and exhort as the Word of God instructs. When the people of God gather in church services, weekly Bible studies, and outreaches, virtue works with your faith to have you there, actively involved. Being a spectator, or an uninvolved saint due to negative past experiences, won't do for the one truly maturing in Christ. Bear in mind Paul's words to forget the past and press forward in Christ. Determine to stay an active, regular, involved contributor to the overall life and health of the church—Christ's body. Every joint is expected to make a contribution (Ephesians 4:16).

Adding virtue to our public walk of faith allows others to access Christ in us, thus they can learn, glean, and be inspired by our example (Philippians 3:17). Faith in Christ is public, to be seen by and inspire hope in all. Virtue is a "PLUS" in the Christian's faith walk, preparing faith for an increase in its partnership and family. It helps faith make room for more—so much more. Faith plus virtue, "PLUS"…

KNOWLEDGE
chapter six

Growing in the knowledge of our Lord Jesus Christ is a process. Faith is the significant foundation upon which we build and grow into the fullness of the stature of Christ. Faith (confidence, trust, conviction) receives and has added to it the distinctive characteristic of virtue (manliness, excellence). Virtue comes to harmonize itself with faith. Into the faith realm, virtue brings along its strength, excellence, courage, and honour. Faith is enlivened, refreshed, and empowered for victory and triumph. The addition of virtue to its mandate of growth in Christ is welcomed and causes faith's mission to be augmented.

Still, there is more. Virtue's task is not a lone one. It has prepared faith to receive yet another comrade, who now approaches for the purpose of working with (not against) faith and virtue. Knowledge comes to aide in the formidable yet glorious directive from heaven to grow in the knowledge of Christ, as Peter so thoroughly presents to the saint of God (2 Peter 1:5–7).

Knowledge is specially made to add and harmonize itself to faith and virtue, who already diligently employ every effort to effectively grow the believer in Christ. How wonderful it is for knowledge to now team itself with faith and virtue. In His infinite wisdom, and timely order, God introduces knowledge to the group. Knowledge, consequently, is a vital element in growing in the knowledge of Jesus Christ. Perhaps this may sound somewhat unnecessary, but Peter's use of the word "knowledge" in his letter is well-placed, for there is a subtle difference between the two words Peter uses for knowledge.

KNOWLEDGE IDENTIFIED

The Word of God is an endlessly rich source of wealth, health, and anything else pertaining to life and godliness. Scripture has much to say about the benefits of godly knowledge in the life of God's people. Here are just a few scriptures on the importance of knowledge:

> *A wise man is strong; yea, a man of knowledge increaseth strength.* (Proverbs 24:5)
> *So that thou incline thine ear unto wisdom, and apply thine heart to understanding; yea, if thou criest after knowledge, and liftest up thy voice for understanding; if thou seekest her as silver, and searchest for her as for hid treasures; then shalt thou understand the fear of the Lord, and find the knowledge of God. For the Lord giveth wisdom: out of his mouth cometh knowledge and understanding.* (Proverbs 2:2–6)
> *In whom are hid all the treasures of wisdom and knowledge.* (Colossians 2:3)

The word "knowledge" comes from the Greek word *epignosis*, which Peter uses in the phrase *"the knowledge of Jesus Christ"* (2 Peter 1:2, 8). We find from Strong's Exhaustive Concordance of the Bible that *epignosis* means "to become thoroughly acquainted with, to know thoroughly, to know accurately, and well."[47] Peter describes for us this

---

[47] Strong, James. *Strong's Exhaustive Concordance of the Bible* (Iowa Falls, IA: Riverside Book and Bible House, 1992), p. 31. See #1921.

Knowledge

type of knowledge in Christ and sets it before us as our goal. Growing into this type of knowledge comes only as we employ diligently all eight of the Christ-like graces in and through our lives.

Peter uses the word "knowledge" a second time within a few verses. Written in English, we may perhaps miss its intended use unless we look into the original Greek to secure its meaning. In 2 Peter 1:5, he uses the Greek word *gnosis* when speaking about the plan to add knowledge to virtue. *Gnosis* means "a seeking to know, an inquiry or investigation."[48] The use of the word knowledge in this way conveys the standard idea of knowledge—that is, to make oneself aware through regular study and experience.

Peter's use of *gnosis* relates to understanding the will of God and His way of salvation through Jesus Christ. Luke draws attention to this very truth in Luke 1:77—*"To give knowledge of salvation unto his people by the remission of their sins."* Paul gives us another look at the same thought in Philippians 3:8—*"Yea doubtless, and I count all things but loss for the excellency of the knowledge of Christ Jesus my Lord: for whom I have suffered the loss of all things, and do count them but dung, that I may win Christ."* New Testament teaching of *gnosis* is that information which brings one to truly know *epignosis*—Jesus Christ. Scripture places a tremendous importance on knowledge and the need for God's people to cultivate and develop it in their lives.

KNOWLEDGE REQUIRED

Throughout scripture, God's expectation of His people is that they have knowledge—*epignosis*. Deuteronomy 6:6–9 reveals this expectation and standard:

> *Memorize his laws and tell them to your children over and over again. Talk about them all the time, whether you're at home or walking along the road or going to bed at night, or getting up in the morning. Write down copies and tie them to your wrists and foreheads to help you obey them. Write these laws on the door frames of your homes and on your town gates. (CEV)*

---

[48] Ibid., p. 31. See #1922.

Michael C. Diotte

By His own declaration, God changes not (Malachi 3:6). His expectations in the Old Testament did not pass away when the New Testament began. 1 Corinthians 10:6–11 teaches that the lessons experienced and learned by God's people in the Old Testament are for our examples. God's standard for His people before the cross of Christ was high—much more than for us, now that we live, move, and have our being in Him (Acts 17:28).

God requires His people to acquire and possess godly knowledge. Growing in the knowledge of Christ Jesus is clearly understood in the scriptures and mandated to the saints of the Most High. The Prophet Jeremiah prophesied about this characteristic being in the New Testament saints. He provides detail about God making a new covenant with His people and writing His laws in their inward parts (the new man in Christ), and in their hearts. Jeremiah says, *"For they shall all know me, from the least of them unto the greatest of them, saith the Lord"* (Jeremiah 31:34). Knowledge is part of the new covenant Christians have with God.

Paul knew the importance of possessing knowledge, and therefore included it as a prayer in his letter to the Colossians:

> *For this cause we also, since the day we heard it, do not cease to pray for you, and to desire that ye might be filled with the knowledge of his will in all wisdom and spiritual understanding; that ye might walk worthy of the Lord unto all pleasing, being fruitful in every good work, and increasing in the knowledge of God.* (Colossians 1:9–10)

Possessing knowledge is pleasing to the Lord. Lack of knowledge leads to ignorance, which is not pleasing to God. Ignorance means to be without education and unaware.[49] Lack of knowledge is a major problem in the body of Christ. According to the Prophet Hosea, many perish for a lack of it (Hosea 4:6), not because knowledge isn't available

---

[49] Encarta World English Dictionary. "Ignorance." Accessed: April 2009 (http://encarta.msn.com/encnet/features/dictionary/DictionaryResults.aspx?le xtype=3&search=ignorance).

Knowledge

but because they rejected knowledge and forgot the law (Word) of God. We see, therefore, it is the responsibility of every Christian to obtain knowledge, study, and show themselves approved unto God (2 Timothy 2:15).

Lack of knowledge is an open door to problems, heartaches, and disasters. If someone doesn't know the benefits they possess as a result of their covenant with God, this world system and the devil can sell them any ideal or philosophy, put God's name on it, and the saint may not know any difference. So many of God's people are suffering and falling short in areas in their lives when God's Word clearly teaches otherwise. Many continue to make excuses for why they cannot study the Word or attend churches that teach the uncompromised Word of the Lord. Satan thrives on excuses and will seize that train of thought and run it straight down the track where the bridge is out.

We are not called to live by the mercy of God; we are called to live and walk by faith. Faith needs knowledge in its life in order to thrive and be victorious over all the works of the enemy. Scripture teaches that there is a judgment upon those who "know" not God and that "obey not" (forget) the gospel of our Lord Jesus Christ (2 Thessalonians 1:8–9). It may be hard to digest, but we must realize that if God places such a high priority and importance upon knowledge, we should do the same.

In Romans 10:1–3, Paul teaches that sincerity and zeal do not impress God unless knowledge is also in the equation. Lack of knowledge, or ignorance, sets one up to seek his or her own righteousness and enter into a life of rebellion against God. With God placing such significance upon obtaining knowledge, where and how should one begin to lay hold of knowledge?

KNOWLEDGE IMMERSION

Only Jesus is the supreme source of true knowledge. In Paul's letter to the Colossians, he reminds the church of this fact and emphasizes this truth by stating, *"In whom are hid all the treasures of wisdom and knowledge"* (Colossians 2:3). To obtain the knowledge scripture speaks about, one must begin with Jesus Christ. Receive Him into your heart, then grow from there into a deep, personal, and intimate relationship with the Saviour and Master of our soul. Without Jesus in first place in your heart and life, the covenant of God is unavailable; its words and teachings will be veiled to any curious onlooker. The truths hidden in the Word of God are available only to those who begin at the cross of Jesus Christ, receiving Him into their heart and life and making Him Lord, the One they will follow.

The Word of God is the only trustworthy source of knowledge and wisdom that is guaranteed to make us wise unto salvation (2 Timothy 3:14–17). We also see that it will make the man of God complete, mature, and lacking nothing. This knowledge is received through studying, meditating, pondering, musing, and muttering the Word of God consistently over and over for the rest of our days on this planet. Joshua 1:8 instructs us to keep the Word of God in our mouth, but also to meditate upon it day and night.

Meditation in the Word of God includes: to ponder, muse, mutter, think about, and study. Adding knowledge to our faith means adding a governing force that generates an atmosphere—or force field, as we might say in modern terminology—around our faith. Knowledge covers our faith like a shield, surrounding it completely. Faith will abide in the realm of knowledge and the shield it provides, thus not being distracted by outside forces. Faith will focus its complete attention on the Word, spending time studying, meditating, musing, pondering, and confessing until God's promises manifest and His will is established on the earth as it is in heaven.

THE KNOWLEDGE TREK

The acquirement of knowledge is a wonderful experience for us to enjoy. Man wants knowledge and seeks to obtain it more and more. Since his temptation in the Garden of Eden, man has craved information, data, and facts about himself, his world, and the universe in which he lives. In the possessing of knowledge one soon realizes that it is not done quickly or magically. Quite the contrary; it is a lifelong commitment. It is a long journey, or a trek. A trek is a journey over a long period of time, usually done by foot (speaking of our walk!), sometimes over rough terrain. Today's society wants everything really fast—as in, yesterday. Nevertheless, God isn't moved by today's society. His methodology is tried and proved. As we therefore yield to His process in acquiring knowledge, we'll soon see and enjoy the benefits.

Having a certain mindset and proper attitude is important in our trek to gain more and grow in the quality of knowledge. Proverbs 2:3–6 teaches us the principle of needing to possess a heart that longs and searches for knowledge like one who is searching for silver and gold. It isn't that God is withholding knowledge from us, it's that God desires to get knowledge over to us. Therefore, it is more about our attitude being properly adjusted when receiving it from the Most High God than it is about Him releasing it to us.

Peter reminds us in 1 Peter 2:2 that *"as newborn babes, [we should] desire the sincere milk of the word, that ye may grow thereby."* Proverbs 8:10–11 gives further insight by stating, *"Receive my instruction, and not silver; and knowledge rather than choice gold. For wisdom is better than rubies; and all the things that may be desired are not to be compared to it."* And later, in Proverbs 12:1: *"Whoso loveth instruction loveth knowledge."*

Our attitude toward knowledge will indeed be a determining factor in our walk with Christ. It would be prudent for the child of God to make Bible reading a daily priority. Seize every available opportunity to study the Word of God and spend time alone with God in His Word. Spend time with others in a corporate setting around God's Word, such as church and Bible studies. Life is short and passing quickly—be sure to carefully weigh the eternal value of the things that crowd and fill your life. If it has no eternal value, then make the necessary adjustments. Remember! You are building something eternal—your life in Christ. Everything else is secondary. Anything apart from the Word of God will pass away.

Recall Paul's words to Timothy in reminding him to give himself totally to the Word of God so that his profiting may be apparent to all, in order to save himself and others that hear him (1 Timothy 4:15–16).

KNOWLEDGE ALERT

Without the proper safeguards in place where our attitudes, mindsets, and hearts are concerned, we can become ensnared by the devil, whose chief goal is to pervert the Word of God, discredit God before the world of men, and humiliate God's people who trust in Him. Without the proper biblical safeguards, we become unyoked from biblical knowledge (unyoked meaning not harnessed correctly with faith, virtue, and the other five graces).

Paul puts in writing for the Corinthians the danger of knowledge unyoked with God and yoked with idols. Simply put, knowledge puffs up (1 Corinthians 8:1–2). It produces arrogance, which is based upon a strong feeling of proud self-importance, and is expressed by treating others with contempt or disregard. Paul reminds the church that knowledge without love is trouble; however, with love we will be edified and know God.

Alexander Pope states, "A little learning is a dangerous thing."[50] Knowledge is only a portion of what we are to learn as believers. There are seven other graces or qualities for us to learn and add to our lives as we grow in Christ. Knowledge needs to be tempered with love and the other six graces so that it may come into its full potential and join with the others to develop us into full, mature, Christ-like beings who bring glory to God and represent Heaven, as becomes ambassadors of Christ.

James 3:13 reads, *"Who is a wise man and endued with knowledge among you? let him shew out of a good conversation his works with meekness of wisdom."* Genuine godly knowledge will manifest itself in a spirit of meekness (teachableness) in a believer's life. If arrogance is manifesting, it is a likely sign that the believer is feeding or associating his knowledge with fear, not faith, and cowardice rather than virtue (manliness). This believer has fallen into the snare of the enemy and become puffed up. If he fails or refuses to repent (change), a fall is inevitable (Proverbs 16:18, 29:23).

Knowledge that works in conjunction with the other seven graces will be a blessing to one's life and walk with the Master. It will minister strength, encouragement, and hope to others in the body of Christ. Knowledge properly applied strengthens our faith, as it feeds upon the Word of God. Our faith will continue to rise to new heights in God

---

[50] Bartleby.com "Alexander Pope." Accessed: March 2009 (http://www.bartleby.com/100/230.99.html).

and we'll grow to be more like Christ Himself. Let us keep our eyes and heart fixed upon the "Word-map" Peter has wonderfully charted before us, so that we may fully grow and mature in the grace and knowledge of our Lord Jesus Christ. We have entered into the amazing mathematical realm of God's Word where life in Christ doesn't end with faith—it begins there, "PLUS" virtue, "PLUS" knowledge, "PLUS"…

TEMPERANCE

chapter seven

Growing is a lifelong commitment. It is a lot of work, requiring a tremendous amount of resources, time, and energy. Growth also has some pain, disappointments, and troubles along the way. However, it is also filled with rewards, treasures, memorable experiences, and lifetime achievements. Growth can and should be *extraordinary*. For Christians, our focus is growth, as Peter succinctly puts it, *"in the knowledge of Jesus Christ* (2 Peter 1:5–8). Growth speaks of increase, development, and expansion. In Isaiah 54:2, we can pull out a few words that speak of God's desire for us to grow—enlarge, stretch, spare not, lengthen, and strengthen. These are powerful words, full of meaning, direction, and encouragement.

In his book, *Laws of Expansion*, Pastor Rick Ciaramitaro speaks about expansion—another word for growth.

Temperance

Expansion is practically living in everything God has prepared for you. It is possessing the ability to do and be everything God calls upon you to do and be. God's desire is to increase you—to transform you from glory to glory. With God there is no barrenness. There is no problem, limitation or circumstance that can dictate your outcome if you are willing to fulfill God's requirement for a fruitful life.[51]

Growth in the knowledge of Jesus Christ is dependent upon having the proper foundation, which is faith (strong conviction and trust) in Jesus Christ not only as Saviour but also Lord of our lives. We saw that Jesus is the chief cornerstone and that faith is the grace that we must first possess, cultivate, and develop in our new life in Christ. To this, we must add as scripture admonishes us to do. We now see a greater importance to faith. It isn't just confessing the Word of God or renewing the mind according to the Word; it is more. It is a culture, a lifestyle, a behaviour. Faith is the very governing force and language of Heaven, and it works… *by love*.

To our faith, we add virtue. Faith doesn't grow alone, according to Bible teaching. It is never faith alone. When it comes to our growth in the knowledge of Christ Jesus, faith requires us to enter the "PLUS" realm of God. Mathematics is God's thing. He loves to add to and multiply in our lives based upon His Word. He subtracts and removes the negatives and adds, increases, and multiplies the positives. He also divides to us the spoils that come from the various battles with the enemy's camp. God loves mathematics and thereby puts "PLUS" into the believer's life of faith. So it is faith "PLUS" virtue (excellence, valour, manliness, courage—that quality that desires to be all that Jesus desires it to be).

We are now growing in the knowledge of Christ, and as we do, God brings more. Now it is faith "PLUS" virtue "PLUS" knowledge (awareness and understanding gained through study and experience—especially regarding the will of God and His way of salvation).

---

[51] Ciaramitaro, Richard. *Laws of Expansion* (Belleville, ON: Guardian Books, 2001), pp. 87–88.

Michael C. Diotte

You may have heard it said, "Two is company—but three is a crowd." Often that is the mindset of the world—but most definitely it's not God's mindset. He does not stop at two or three. He works on the principle found in Ephesians 3:20, which is basically this—so much more than ever before. Therefore, God's mathematics continues with faith "PLUS" virtue "PLUS" knowledge "PLUS" temperance (self-control or self-restraint).

SELF-RESTRAINT

It seems logical and right that if anything should be added to the current equation—faith "PLUS" virtue "PLUS" knowledge—it should be temperance. Temperance is that quality or influence that will help us to handle knowledge correctly and wisely. If we fail to have the ability to properly use knowledge where our faith and virtue are concerned, we may find ourselves steeped in a whole new realm of problems we are not prepared to face. Please understand that, throughout our entire growth in Christ process, we must never presume we have arrived. The Apostle Paul summarizes it this way: *"Brethren, I count not myself to have apprehended: but this one thing I do, forgetting those things which are behind, and reaching forth unto those things which are before"* (Philippians 3:13). He is basically saying, "We're not in heaven yet, so don't get a big head about where you are in your growth process in Christ. Just keep on going. There is much, much more to grasp."

Therefore, with this in mind, let us bring temperance on board our journey of growth in the knowledge of Christ, which began first and foremost with faith in Christ. To do this, we must better understand what temperance is and how to add it to our daily living for Christ. We have an opportunity to make temperance a "PLUS" in our lives, one that will stretch us and take us into places in Christ and His Word that are higher and farther above anywhere we've ever been before.

The Greek word for temperance (self-control) is *enkrateia*, which is from the root word *kratos*, meaning "strength." Temperance speaks of the ability to master one's own desires and passions, bringing them into subjection to Christ. Bible Commentator Edgar V. McKnight says of

Temperance

temperance, "Where this virtue subsists (abides), temptation can have little influence."[52]

God's Word expounds on the subject of temperance, revealing that it is coupled with righteousness (God's expected standard for man) and self-control, which is man's response to God's standard (Acts 24:25). Galatians 5:23 reveals self-control to be a fruit of the Spirit—thus, one who walks in the Spirit will bear this fruit in their lives. In writing to Titus, Paul teaches that self-control is required of those who serve as elders in the church (Titus 1:8). In our main text of 2 Peter 1:6, self-control follows immediately after knowledge, indicating that what is learned must be put into practice. Thus, self-control is the discipline and alignment of one's self to live in harmony with God's Word and the qualities of faith, virtue, and knowledge.

SELF-DISCIPLINE FOR CHRIST'S DISCIPLES

No matter what our thoughts, excuses, or attitudes toward the subject of self-control, nothing is going to change the reality of God's expectations toward us. No amount of praying, fasting, or complaining is going to change God's mind on the matter. In Luke's gospel, we learn that denial of self is going to be a way of life for the one who follows Jesus (Luke 9:23). God's grace instructs us that self-control is necessary in order to live a godly and righteous life (Titus 2:11–12). In order to be a disciple of Jesus Christ, self-control must be understood.

Paul understood the necessity of self-control operating in the lives of believers. He writes to the saints at Corinth about the value of temperance and uses himself as an example to learn from. *"But I keep under my body, and bring it into subjection: lest that by any means, when I have preached to others, I myself should be a castaway"* (1 Corinthians 9:27). The force and quality of temperance at work in our lives will keep us from becoming castaways. A castaway is someone who has been shipwrecked or set adrift. For the believer, this would mean being set adrift from our faith in Christ. Paul put this thought in writing for

---

[52] Biblestudyguide.org "Growing in the Knowledge of Christ: Controlling the Self." Accessed: May 2010 (http://www.biblestudyguide.org/ebooks/copeland/know.PDF).

Michael C. Diotte

Timothy and the saints of God: *"Holding faith, and a good conscience; which some having put away concerning faith have made shipwreck* (1 Timothy 1:19). The force of temperance will keep you walking well in the faith and your conscience clear.

With so much happening these days, the saint of God must simply be vigilant in the Word of God and keep their heart focused, fixed, and fastened to Jesus. There is no need for the children of God to spend time everyday speaking and concerning themselves with how bad the world is getting. Jesus already told us this was going to happen (Matthew 24). Paul told Timothy that the latter days were going to be filled with all kinds of happenings (1 Timothy 4). God raises certain ones up who are called to keep us well informed of what is happening in the world and what and how the church should respond to it. We don't really need to spend so much time looking to the world's media for information that is already negative and tainted with hopelessness and despair.

We need to make a fresh commitment to focus upon what truly matters for each of us as God's children—that being the development and maturing of our Christ-like nature and the strengthening of our faith. *"Let your light so shine before men, that they may see your good works, and glorify your Father which is in heaven"* (Matthew 5:16).

Remember what Paul explained to us about the behaviour of an athlete? In 1 Corinthians 9, he puts into plain words the need for self-control in our lives as Christians. Paul compares our Christian growth with that of an athlete in training for the Olympics. *"And every man that striveth for the mastery is temperate in all things. Now they do it to obtain a corruptible crown; but we an incorruptible"* (1 Corinthians 9:25). We therefore learn from Paul that just as an athlete must employ self-control to win the race, we must also employ with all diligence the same quality in order to obtain an imperishable crown.

Sharon Daugherty, anointed psalmist, teacher, and author, adds:

> Paul was making a comparison between the Olympic games of his day and the spiritual race of the Christian… we must have the same compelling determination for highest excellence as a Christian as the Olympic athlete has for his endeavors.

Temperance

It is not enough to be an "average Christian." Paul exhorts us to be "above average." He exhorts us to seek excellence. This excellence can be achieved only through self-control.[53]

Some say that the controlling of the self is easier said than done. However real that line of thinking may be to them, truth be known, employing the quality of self-control isn't really that difficult when we do it God's way, as we'll see.

EMPLOYING SELF-CONTROL

Life, growth, and existence on planet earth afford each of us with plenty of challenges. Scripture acknowledges the challenge we face in this area of employing temperance. Proverbs 16:32 states, *"Better a patient man than a warrior, a man who controls his temper than one who takes a city"* (NIV) In essence, it is easier to capture a whole city than for a person who has no self-control to lead or rule his own life. As Christians, we are still human beings living in a fallen world. This world system isn't supposed to have dominion over us or influence us in negative ways. It will try to regain control over our lives so that we are hindered or totally stopped from growing in the knowledge of Christ Jesus. Christ, however, has completed the work of redemption, having lifted us up to a place in Himself that is far above all principality, power, might, and dominion, as seen in Ephesians 1:21–22, and placed all these things and more under our feet.

We can and do get ourselves into some precarious situations as Christians because we fail to exercise self-control (self-restraint). Sometimes it is plain laziness that brings on our troubles, and other times it is from being careless with our words. The Apostle James addressed this very matter in his letter to the saints of God regarding self-control, our tongues, and the words we speak: *"If any man among you seem to be religious, and bridleth not his tongue, but deceiveth his own heart, this man's religion is vain"* (James 1:26).

---

[53] Daugherty, Sharon. *Walking in the Spirit—A Fruitful Life* (Tulsa, OK: Harrison House, 1984), p. 92.

Michael C. Diotte

James knew how much trouble our tongue could get us into. He goes on James 3:2–10 to expound on the depth of trouble a tongue can create, and likens the tongue to an out of control fire. We quickly learn the need for self-control in the believer's life. Satan would enjoy nothing more than to see us sabotage our own lives simply by being careless and not employing self-control. Most of what we blame the devil for could perhaps be blamed on us for not properly and diligently employing the grace of self-control in our lives and in the situations we face.

We all have similar challenges in this regard. If you have lived on this planet for any length of time, you'll discover that—pronto. Paul teaches this very thing in Romans 7:14–25, by giving illustrations from his own life both before and after Christ. Paul reveals through his own testimony the need for self-control and dependency upon Christ. He shares personal experiences and the frustration of dealing with oneself. He knows what it is like to try and live under the law, to want to do right but end up doing wrong. It truly is a battle we all face while in this flesh. Yet he doesn't end it there, leaving us hanging in despair and filled with hopelessness. Paul's words and writings to us are anything but dark and hopeless.

So, if the battle rages on, how do we bring ourselves under the influence of self-control? What does God's Word say and reveal that will help us? The answer, of course, is always abundantly clear: the Bible has solid encouragement and clear, helpful instructions for us so that we may be successful for God's glory. It isn't as hard as some may make it out to be.

Scripture acknowledges the battle between both the spirit and the flesh, as evidenced in Galatians 5:16–17. Peter validates this thought in 1 Peter 2:11. As long as we are on this earth, a battle will be waged over the soul (mind, emotions, will, and intellect). Why? Satan knows that whoever controls or has the most influence on the soul of man (his mind, emotions, will, and intellect) can control or influence man's destiny. God's Word gives hope! Paul reveals this hope in Romans 7:24–25, when overwhelmed by the condition of the flesh part of man (note that he is *not* referring to the newborn creature in Christ), he states, "*What a wretched man I am! Who will rescue me from this <u>body</u>*

Temperance

of death? Thanks be to God—through Jesus Christ our Lord!" (NIV) He acknowledges the fight and the intensity of the battle in the flesh, but he immediately offers hope and gives a strong reminder of where our focus should be and remain—in thanksgiving to God, through Jesus Christ our Lord!

Paul moves us from the battle described in Romans 7 on to another aspect of our journey of discovery in Romans 8. Too many get stuck in a Romans 7 experience and forget to forge ahead to Romans 8, where there is more. Paul takes us right into life in the Spirit and in Christ by explaining immediately with profound clarity that in Christ *"there is therefore now no condemnation to them which are in Christ Jesus, who walk not after the flesh, but after the Spirit"* (Romans 8:1). He continues to encourage us: *"Therefore, brethren, we are debtors, not to the flesh, to live after the flesh"* (Romans 8:12).

How then can this be so? Galatians 5:24 continues, *"And they that are Christ's have crucified the flesh with the affections and lusts."* Paul acknowledges the problem as being a very real one; however, he also reveals the solution for the Christian who finds himself in such a state. Simply put: crucify the flesh along with the lust and affections of the flesh. The solution is always found in Christ and His Word.

THE WAY OUT

Scripture teaches that there is always a way of escape (see 1 Corinthians 10:13). Paul, however, gives clear insight for the believer concerning this matter of winning over the dictates of the flesh (employing self-control). In Romans 6:3–6, he explains to us the need to properly identify ourselves with Christ's death and resurrection. First, there is a need to truly realize that our body of sin is now put to death in Christ. We are immersed with Him in His death, and also now have risen in the likeness of His resurrection. Now in His resurrection, we live free from the control of the flesh and all of its appetites. Paul does also remind us that we must choose. Always, it is our choice—God doesn't force His freedom and liberty upon anyone (see Romans 6:12–13).

Scripture doesn't say that Christians will no longer be tempted, but it does emphasize that sin's authority, dominion, and rule no longer is over us (Romans 6:14). Paul contrasts for us the one who is outside of Christ in Romans 7 to the one who is in Christ in Romans 8. For the one outside of Christ, we see in Romans 7:23–24 the pull on the flesh man. For the one ruled by the flesh, captivity to its dictates and lusts is inevitable. Again, Paul contrasts clearly for us the one who now is in Christ. Romans 6:12 says, *"Let not sin therefore reign in your mortal body, that ye should obey it in the lusts thereof."* The choice is clearly ours. Keep in mind—now that we are in Christ, any battle we face is winnable. How so? Christ has already won the war and given us the victory (1 John 5:4).

Thus, now that we are immersed in Christ through baptism, we continue on to live our lives in Christ, being led and guided by the Holy Spirit (John 16:13), which is into all truth. Romans 8:13 says, *"For if ye live after the flesh, ye shall die: but if ye through the Spirit do mortify the deeds of the body, ye shall live."* Allowing the Holy Spirit to lead us will take us into more life than we could ever imagine. He will take us into everything that Jesus said would be available for us, if only we will follow. If we will devote our time to fellowshipping with the Holy Spirit and following His lead, we will discover how easy it is to walk victoriously in this earth as Jesus promised. Galatians 5:16 bears this out by saying, *"This I say then, Walk in the Spirit, and ye shall not fulfil the lust of the flesh."* The Holy Spirit leads us as we set our minds upon the Word of God (Romans 8:5).

Again, John 16:13 reveals this as one of His purposes—to lead and direct us into all truth. To the degree that our minds are fixed upon the Word of God, the Holy Spirit will be able to lead us. The Holy Spirit will not only lead and guide us into all truth, He will also help us to live a life empowered by the Spirit. Philippians 4:13 reminds us that we can do it all—through Christ which strengthens us. Philippians 2:13 says, *"For it is God which worketh in you both to will and to do of his good pleasure."* God's power is working in us, and according to Paul in Ephesians 3:16–21, we have ahead of us a life full of empowerment that in the end will bring glory to Christ Jesus forever.

The Holy Spirit empowers our lives as we dwell in the Word, establishing our hearts by faith, becoming rooted and grounded

(Ephesians 3:17). He also empowers us in our inner man (Ephesians 3:16) as we commune with Him. The Spirit-led Christian is promised a Spirit-empowered life, and this is done through God's Word and prayer. We are strengthened through our relationship and communion with the Holy Spirit, Who was sent from the Father in heaven, in Jesus' Name, to be with us. Thus, as we persist in keeping the flesh crucified through our union with Christ, allowing the Holy Spirit to consistently lead us and empower us, self-control (or the force of temperance) will become natural and an abundant grace in our life. Self-control is a valued partner with faith, virtue, and knowledge. The fruitfulness of the Spirit-led and Spirit-controlled life will be seen even more so in our lives. Christ's character and nature will become clearer for all to see, leading us to find hope and freedom through a personal relationship with Him. Being like Him in this earth is our focus and destiny.

PRINCIPLES OF SELF-CONTROL

God's Word lays out for us some key principles and guidelines in the implementation of self-control (temperance) in our growth in the knowledge of Christ. Paul states by his own example, in 1 Corinthians 9:27, that we must keep our body under and bring it into subjection. In his letter to Titus, Paul says we must deny ungodliness and worldly lusts, living soberly, righteously, and godly in this present world (Titus 2:12). Paul also gives a similar admonishment to Timothy in 2 Timothy 2:22.

Now that we are in and growing in Christ—we are not to be in bondage to anything (see 1 Corinthians 6:12). Self-control properly employed in our lives will help us to deny ourselves so that we may be of service to others around us (see Philippians 2:3–4, 1 Corinthians 8:9–13, and Romans 14:14–21). We learn that maintaining control over oneself applies not only to one's body, but also to one's ego.

Paul does also warn about a false self-control that is birthed out of religious ideas, human traditions, or ignorance of God's ways. A look at Colossians 2:20–23 and 1 Timothy 4:1–5 will reveal to us man's attempts to exercise his version of self-control based upon his traditions and mindsets. It may all look and feel good, but in the end it is an imposter to the grace of temperance that comes to help our faith, virtue, and knowledge so that we may continue to grow in the knowledge of our Lord Jesus Christ.

A life led and empowered by the Holy Spirit will continue to see more added to our lives for God's glory. Our faith enjoys life in the "PLUS" realm that God has opened up for us through life in His Word and His Spirit. Controlling the "self" is an automatic progression in our growth process in Christ. Faith needs the force of temperance to assist the team in its purpose to enter into the fullness of the stature of Christ. Self-control brings meaning to faith. It keeps virtue (excellence) disciplined and on target. Self-control (temperance) keeps knowledge out of the realm of becoming merely an academic exercise resulting in a puffed-up mind.

Growing in the knowledge of Jesus Christ becomes all the more thrilling and exciting when we live it immersed in and empowered by the Holy Spirit. Walking in the Spirit, in the realm of the Holy Ghost, allows us to easily access the force of temperance and maintain it as a vital member of the team of the graces now at work in our lives. As we properly let temperance flow in our lives in Christ, we'll do well to steer clear of human traditions and the habits of a fallen world.

Faith in Christ (the chief cornerstone) will continue to resonate with joy and God-like enthusiasm as each God-designed "PLUS" steps into our growth process to add aspects to the dimension of our faith that will cause it to be the envy and talk of the world. It only gets better as we step further into the fascinating realm God has had for us all along… the realm of "PLUS," which begins with faith… "PLUS" virtue… "PLUS" knowledge… "PLUS" temperance… "PLUS"…

PATIENCE: *Bearing Up Under Trials*

chapter eight

Growing in the knowledge of Jesus Christ is a most marvellous pursuit. We have observed in our study that our growth begins with faith (strong conviction and trust in Christ). There begins our entrance into God's "PLUS" realm. Faith "PLUS" virtue (excellence, valour, and manliness) "PLUS" knowledge (regarding God's will, "PLUS" temperance (self-control, mastering one's desires and passions)… and now we welcome our next grace team member—Patience.

Various translations depict the word "patience" as perseverance and cheerful steadfastness. Consequently, we can perhaps see the advent of patience to our growth coming at an excellent point in time. The Greek word for perseverance is *hupomone*, which literally means "an abiding under." Strong's Concordance defines perseverance as "cheerful or hopeful endurance."[54] This implies that a series of events may happen that require

---

[54] Strong, James. *Strong's Exhaustive Concordance of the Bible* (Iowa Falls, IA: Riverside Book and Bible House, 1992), p. 74. See #5281.

us to wait, endure, and be determined to go through a process in order to grow, mature, and develop into all that God desires for us.

A prevailing attitude or understanding that some people have regarding patience is that it is a passive grace that just puts up with whatever may come its way. Many Christians believe or have been taught that we must just accept what comes our way as the will of God for our lives. Some may even begin to sing the well-known secular song, "Que Sera, Sera—Whatever Will Be, Will Be." However, patience doesn't just wait for the storm to pass, hoping that there will be little or no damage. Neither does godly patience succumb to attacks in the hopes of pleasing God or fulfilling some unknown purpose He may have for our lives (this subject in and of itself would stand as a complete study). Suffice to say, whether passing through a storm or dealing with an all-out enemy attack, patience acts as an anchor for the soul secured in the Word of God, while at the same time manoeuvring through the event with cheerful steadfastness and endurance, confident of this one thing—that God is working this out for our good.

Patience is an active grace involved with the team of graces already at work in our lives. Its arrival is designed to harmonize with the ongoing efforts of the team to bring us into full conformity to the image of Christ. It brings with it the quality of being able to press on through to its destination despite the obstacles it faces. Patience refuses to "grin and bear it," but goes beyond that attitude toward a hearty, cheerful endurance that praises and thanks God in spite of surrounding circumstances. Proverbs 17:22 says, *"A merry heart doeth good like a medicine."* The force of patience seeks to keep the atmosphere filled with cheer—almost like a morale officer. Bible commentator Adam Clarke notes, "Patience bears all trials and difficulties with an even mind, enduring in all, and persevering through all."[55] Thus, patience doesn't simply bear with trials; it actually bears up under the trial.

Patience is a quality and grace required in all Christians, and Jesus demonstrates this grace for us in His life:

---

[55] Studylight.org. "The Adam Clarke Commentary: The Second General Epistle of Peter." Accessed: April 2009 (http://www.studylight.org/com/acc/view.cgi?book=2pe&chapter=001).

Patience: Bearing Up Under Trials

Wherefore seeing we also are compassed about with so great a cloud of witnesses, let us lay aside every weight, and the sin which doth so easily beset us, and let us run with patience the race that is set before us. Looking unto Jesus the author and finisher of our faith; who for the joy that was set before him endured the cross, despising the shame, and is set down at the right hand of the throne of God. (Hebrews 12:1–2)

Paul demonstrates patience in his own life and shares with us the experience when writing to Timothy:

But thou hast fully known my doctrine, manner of life, purpose, faith, longsuffering, charity, patience, persecutions, afflictions, which came unto me at Antioch, at Iconium, at Lystra; what persecutions I endured: but out of them all the Lord delivered me. (2Timothy 3:10-11)

Again, the Word of God presupposes patience as a necessity in our everyday life. It is the stick-to-it, optimistically cheerful force on the team.

PATIENCE'S CODE OF CONDUCT

Patience wasn't commissioned by God to be a curse in our lives. More exactly, patience's appearance upon the grace team is for the purpose of maturing our character in Christ. James 1:4 expresses it this way: *"But let patience have her perfect work, that ye may be perfect and entire, wanting nothing."* Jesus, Himself teaches the following: *"But that on the good ground are they, which in an honest and good heart, having heard the word, keep it, and bring forth fruit with patience"* (Luke 8:15). The Master stresses the need for us to employ patience in our lives. We see by His teaching that patience is an important grace to have actively operating in the realm of God's Word in our lives. Patience is required in the lives of believers in order for them to bear fruit.

Patience, also known as cheerful perseverance, is the right grace to have when faced with a trial that seems to go on and on and on. Patience assisted and worked with the faith of the Thessalonians when they were faced with troubles and hardships, helping them to endure persecutions and trials. The force of patience (perseverance) also assisted Job to endure his nine months of hardships and difficulties:

> *Behold, we count them happy which endure. Ye have heard of the patience of Job, and have seen the end of the Lord; that the Lord is very pitiful, and of tender mercy.* (James 5:11)

For those who would identify themselves with Job and his experience, claiming they are in the same class of experience as he was, keep this in mind—Job's experience included the total and complete loss of his wealth, the death of his children, and the onset of disease. Throughout the entire experience—which lasted nine months—scripture teaches that Job remained patient, which is that cheerful endurance which bears up under trial. Job also refused to believe anything negative about God and steadied his faith with the force of patience.

Trials, tests, and temptations are part and parcel to living on this planet and in the fallen world system. They come to us all—that's a guarantee. However, their often surprising arrivals into the daily routines of our lives need not poison our hearts, minds, attitudes, and behaviours with negative and bitter influence. As we continue to thoroughly utilize the grace of patience in our lives, allowing it to become an effective member of the team of graces already present, we will steady our course and development and be in a position to receive what God has promised, as seen in Hebrews 10:36—*"For ye have need of patience, that, after ye have done the will of God, ye might receive the promise."*

Romans 2:7 explains that patience is linked to glory, honour and eternal things: *"To them who by patient continuance in well doing seek for glory and honour and immortality, eternal life."* Patience, indeed, is a valued and most welcomed grace in our ongoing pursuit to grow in the knowledge of Christ Jesus (2 Peter 1:8). How does one add, cultivate, and allow patience to work in their life? The Word of God always has the answers and direction we need in order to be successful in any undertaking.

MATURING PATIENCE

Romans 15:4–5 brings to us a remarkable word of encouragement:

For whatsoever things were written aforetime were written for our learning, that we through patience and comfort of the scriptures might have hope. Now the God of patience and consolation grant you to be likeminded one toward another according to Christ Jesus.

God's very Word is the provider of patience. It is through the scriptures that we gain patience and our hope comes alive. God, being also the God of patience, expects us to demonstrate the same cheerful, endurance (patience, perseverance) with one another in the body of Christ.

Romans 8:25 says that while we are yet in faith, hoping (Bible hope) for what we currently do not see, we do so with patience and wait for its manifestation. Patience steadies us in our faith, to stay on target until the manifestation of what we have believed and hoped for comes to pass. In Colossians 1:11 Paul says, *"Strengthened with all might, according to his glorious power, unto all patience and longsuffering with joyfulness."* Here we see patience expanded in our thinking to include longsuffering *with* joyfulness. That's the company that attitude and patience consistently keep.

Romans 5:3 shows that our attitude during tribulations should be one of glory, understanding and knowing that tribulation works patience. While on this earth, patience will never be unemployed. It will never need to be laid off due to no work. Quite the contrary! These days, perseverance (patience) will seemingly be more active than ever before.

The quality of patience is one of cheerful, joyful optimism. The trial may even grow to be increasingly difficult as the days pass, but that will not bother patience; it will make the adjustment continue to feed on the Word of God and keep the atmosphere cheery and ready for everyone to break out in songs of praise to God. James, a servant of God (James 1:1), reveals to us that when tests, trials, or tribulations come against your faith, patience (with its ability to persevere, be longsuffering, and cheerful) immediately begins to work (be employed) to steady our faith (James 1:4). James notes that patience's entire meaning lacks nothing and is fully equipped for the task at hand. Patience is committed to the total success of your faith. Its presence on the team is to ensure your faith wins.

PATIENCE'S VIEW

Patience doesn't see the task that faith has embarked upon—of growing in the knowledge of Christ Jesus—to be one of vanity or hopelessness. Like faith, patience can see the end result (which includes looking unto Jesus, the Author and Finisher of our faith) and sets itself to running the race set before it (Hebrews 12:1–4). As believers, we are encouraged to consider Jesus and what hostility He endured for our sakes. He didn't grumble, murmur, or complain. Ephesians 5:1 reminds us to be an imitator of Him (God), like dear children. Even the prophets of old patiently endured the afflictions that came upon them (James 5:10–11). Hebrews 11:32–38 gives a brief list of many other things that the saints of old patiently endured, thereby helping us to remember that many of the things we complain about today are often nowhere near what the saints in days past had to endure. Even if some of the things we have to endure are weightier and more difficult by comparison, the force of patience comes to us fully equipped (see James 1:4) to handle whatever needs to be handled so that faith may continue to work, grow, and mature, as it is destined to do.

Patience's view is quite different from ours, if we are not viewing things the way God does. Patience always sees things the way God's Word does. Again, it doesn't know how to be negative—it is the morale officer of the team. It remains upbeat about everything. It is natural for God's people to encourage one another (Hebrews 3:12–14), to be optimistic, to assemble together with one another to provoke each other to do good things and remain in love (Hebrews 10:24–25).

Every time God's people avoid each other—staying away from church, Bible studies, prayer groups, outreaches, etc.—Satan gains the upper hand and starts his work of sowing seeds of discord, mistrust, hurts, unforgiveness, resentment, and bitterness. Patience knows the value of teamwork, hence it knows the value of all of us assembling together regularly to keep each other accountable, encouraged, strengthened, and especially feeling loved. Patience's attitude and view is one of joy. No matter what the grace team encounters or falls into, patience sees it as another opportunity to release more joy into the atmosphere—and why not? God remains on the throne, Jesus retains the victory, and the Holy Spirit is present with us to keep this truth before us as saints of the Most High God.

Patience enjoys a good workout. It sees tests, trials, and tribulations like that of another trip to the gym. It's an opportunity to strengthen and develop its muscle mass and to tone up the team so that it is fit as a fiddle to run the race set before it. This isn't a brief stint, but a marathon. Therefore, patience sees all challenges as opportunities to take another step forward to overall better health for the whole man (spirit, soul, and body). It has the finish line in sight and plans to help the team (and yourself) to have an abundant entrance into the kingdom when all is said and done (2 Peter 1:11).

Patience encourages the team to go into a trial with some excitement and anticipation because it knows the Holy Ghost is there to help us. No matter what happens, patience knows that no shame will come upon us, for the Holy Ghost will shed God's love throughout our hearts (Romans 5:3–5). It'll keep the team looking forward (2 Corinthians 4:16-18). The challenges we go through are only for a moment—just wait until you see what is waiting for you on the other side. Hallelujah! So, Christian, take heart, be encouraged, and learn to encourage yourself at all times. There will be days, and maybe even whole seasons, where staying charged up for the Lord is easier said than done, but don't allow your heart and mind to entertain a "give-up" mindset.

Be even more resolved to press through—come what may. We're not in this because of the reward! We're in it because of love! Love will hold you on target and get you through when material or natural things will give up.

Faith and its team understand the cost, commitment, and all that is involved in seeing something through. They've counted themselves in for the duration. Perseverance truly manifests when we press forward in doing good (God's Word). It will rise up and assist you to overcome when persisting temptations hound your mind and body in an effort to side-track your faith. Patience, if you will let it, will help you to turn your back on temptations or those things that easily beset you. It will want to sing praise to God and be joyful right in the midst of difficulty. Many Christians think it strange to have a song of praise rise up within their heart at difficult times and trials in their lives, but that's the Holy Ghost working with the force of patience to sustain them.

Patience is like self-control in that it is a daily exercise. It knows that this exercise is for today, tomorrow, and every other day after that. Paul said in 2 Thessalonians 3:5, *"And the Lord direct your hearts into the love of God, and into the patient waiting for Christ."* Patience knows that it could be awhile. Waiting is involved. It will allow the Holy Ghost to direct you into the love of God so that you will enjoy the journey. Patience has a portfolio of psalms, hymns, and spiritual songs—along with melodies for the heart and much giving of thanks to the Lord—available for the journey (Ephesians 5:19–20). So let patience have its maturing work in you. Don't stop this powerful grace from doing what it knows to do—growing in the knowledge of Christ Jesus—a lot more joyful and glorious. Hear Paul's words to Timothy in 1 Timothy 6:11, to *"follow after righteousness, godliness, faith, love, patience, meekness."* Nurturing the quality of cheerful perseverance in our lives as we grow, giving it freedom to enhance the team already in place—faith, virtue, knowledge, and temperance—allows us to become *"steadfast, unmoveable, always abounding in the work of the Lord, forasmuch as ye know that your labour is not in vain in the Lord"* (1 Corinthians 15:58).

According to God's Word, patience's expertise dramatically augments the team's work and task of growing us in the knowledge of Jesus Christ (2 Peter 1:8). Patience launches us forward, supporting our faith with cheerful rejoicing, lifting our eyes to stand as Abram did once before with God, Who asked him to look to the north, south, east, and west and said, *"For all the land which thou seest, to thee will I give it, and to thy seed for ever"* (Genesis 13:15). From that day forward, Abram stepped into God's "PLUS" realm, never looking back. He realized then that he wasn't simply choosing natural land to dwell in, but a permanent, eternal position in God's realm, thus securing for him and his posterity more than they could ever think or imagine.

He simply believed God that day, stepped forward in faith, and grew from there. Abram became Abraham, who became the father of faith. Doors forever opened to God's "PLUS" realm. Can you see it? Just like Abram did—faith "PLUS" virtue "PLUS" knowledge "PLUS" temperance "PLUS" patience. Growth in Christ has become so incredible, yet there's so much more… because before us is yet another "PLUS"…

GODLINESS: Seeking to Please God

chapter nine

We are becoming more and more like Christ Jesus. 2 Peter 1:5–7 is an awesome blueprint of our image in Christ. Growing in the knowledge of Christ, as 2 Peter 1:5–7 indicates, requires effort. As believers, we employ every bit of diligence we can muster in order to harmonize, add, and work the graces together properly so that we may grow well in Christ. Each grace diligently works in conjunction with the others, growing and moving us to become like Christ, exemplifying His Christ-like character in our own lives so that the world may see Jesus in us and catch a glimpse of Heaven.

We remember the reasons and motivations for us to grow in the knowledge of Jesus Christ:
1) Grace and peace will be multiplied.
2) We will receive and have access to all things pertaining to life and godliness.
3) We'll avoid spiritual short-sightedness and amnesia.

4) We'll have an abundant entrance into the everlasting kingdom of God.

The development of Christ's character in us from the point of new birth begins, without a doubt, with the foundation of faith (conviction, trust, belief). To our faith, we begin to employ the force of diligence.

Meticulously, the Apostle Peter takes us step by step through the development process in Christ. Once we are established in our faith, Peter moves us to add virtue (excellence, valour, and manliness), knowledge (increasing in knowledge regarding God's will), temperance (self-control, the mastering of one's desires and passions), and patience (perseverance to cheerfully bear up under the trial or temptation). We should now pause and carefully note what is linked to patience and added to the team of graces already diligently employed in growing us in the knowledge of Christ—godliness!

GODLINESS CHARACTERIZED

Bible teacher Mark A. Copeland comments on *eusebia,* the Greek word for "godliness." He says that its literal meaning is "to worship well… to be very devout."[56] Godliness denotes piety characterized by a strong respectful belief toward God, which also includes seeking to be well-pleasing to Him. The governing factors in godliness will be love and a reverential awe of respect from the heart toward God. Entering now to join forces with the grace team, godliness follows perseverance. Its attitude, as we have just seen portrayed from the Greek, is one of reverence toward God. Paul shows us in 1 Timothy 6:3 that the wholesome words and teachings of our Lord Jesus Christ are according to godliness. It is *"profitable unto all things, having promise of the life that now is, and of that which is to come"* (1 Timothy 4:8). We see Peter acknowledging this also from our study of 2 Peter 1:3.

Godliness keeps our focus upon God, keeping in check our motivation for doing what we do. Without godliness added to our faith

---

[56] Executable Outlines. "Growing in the Knowledge of Jesus Christ: Seeking to Please God." Accessed: May 2009 (http://executableoutlines.com/know/know_07.htm).

and its covenant partners, we may do a lot of right or good things, but possibly for the wrong reasons. It is therefore imperative to keep a proper reverence and focus upon God.

WARNING

Scripture does issue a warning about a counterfeit form of godliness or piety. There are many who purely do not understand that the godliness they are operating in, or the piety they are demonstrating, is hypocritical and not pleasing to God. Paul explains and issues a warning to the church in 2 Timothy 3:1-5, describing a group that will have a form of godliness but deny its very power, authority, and jurisdiction to operate in their lives. Paul portrays these individuals as "lovers of pleasure" rather than "lovers of God." This is an outward form and is employed only to impress others so that one may exalt himself and gain more attention.

Jesus also issues a warning to His disciples about this counterfeit godliness, which He labels as hypocrisy in Matthew 6:1-18. We learn from Jesus and His Word that true godliness is not characterized by outward shows. Godliness flows from the inward man, influencing the attitudes and behaviours of an individual so that Christ's character is revealed for others to see. Again, godliness works with the team to ensure a right devotion to God, desiring and seeking to please only Him. Without this focus, godliness is reduced to mere piety without power, which is hypocrisy as far as God is concerned.

GODLY CONDUCT

Being a disciple of Jesus is a high calling. It isn't easy or for lazy, self-absorbed people. Godliness puts its entire attention upon God, desiring above all else to delight Him. Jesus makes an amazing statement in John 8:29 about His relationship with the Father, that He, Jesus, always did what pleased Him. We discover in Galatians 1:10 those who desire to please man cannot be servants of God. The means by which we could please God was integrated into the teachings of the apostles as a commandment and was harmonized with the believer's walk before God, as seen in 1 Thessalonians 4:1-2. What greater purpose can there be than to please God? Jesus taught, lived, and demonstrated this for us to follow.

GAIN AND PROFIT

As the newest member to the grace team, godliness brings with it a tremendous wealth and benefit to raise our growth in the knowledge of Christ to a new dimension of beauty, worth, strength, and other desirable heavenly qualities that will bring great gain (1 Timothy 6:6) to the kingdom of God in the earth and to the believer's life in Christ. It is worth repeating Paul's words to Timothy about the value of godliness—that it is, indeed, *"profitable unto all things"* (1 Timothy 4:).

The Word of God emphasizes that the profit of God's Word will be seen in our lives immediately, given that we put the Word and God's kingdom first place in our lives. According to Matthew 6:33, if we'll seek God's kingdom and His righteousness, *"all these things shall be added unto [us]."* When asked by the disciples about having left all for the gospel's sake, Jesus responded, *"He shall receive an hundredfold now in this time... and in the world to come eternal life"* (Mark 10:30). It does the believer well to remember the promises of God so that they may find comfort and encouragement from the scriptures during difficult seasons of testing. Romans 6:22 reminds us that we are free from sin, and that the fruit we bear is unto holiness, and the end everlasting life.

We are exhorted by Peter to give diligence to holy living according to the promises (Word) of God (2 Peter 3:10–14) and to remain diligent in such things so that we are found of Him in peace, without spot, and blameless. The quality of godliness will keep us focused on this aspect of our growth in the knowledge of Jesus Christ.

Godliness actively working in a believer's life will truly prosper them in a way that has merit and significance, and which will bring glory to God and His Name. Godliness produces and gives power to the believer's life and faith. In his letter to Timothy, Paul said that there were those who had a form of godliness but were actually denying its power (2 Timothy 3:15). We learn from Paul's letter and statement here that true godliness has power. The one whose conduct and communication is pleasing to God will be empowered by Him. God will work in us both to will and do of His good pleasure (Philippians 2:13).

We are not left alone to figure out how to live godly lives. God is working right there in us, faithfully giving oversight to His Word to bring it to pass. His purpose is to strengthen us, beginning with the inner man (Ephesians 3:16). Remember—we have been speaking and learning about God's "PLUS" realm. There is just so much more for the believer to experience, learn, and grow in. Paul gives us a glimpse of this in Ephesians 3:20; I call it the so-much-more-than-ever-before realm. However, during our study, we'll simplify it and call it God's "PLUS" realm.

> *Now unto him that is able to do exceeding abundantly above all that we ask or think, according to the power that worketh in us* (Ephesians 3:20)

Godliness is the key which opens the door to God's power, enabling us to live faith-filled lives free of Satan's agenda and far above the world's fallen system. Like the other qualities of grace being added into the growth process of our lives, godliness needs to likewise be added. Paul explained to Timothy, his son in the faith, that godliness in our lives needs to be exercised in order for it to bring the benefits of a godly life (1 Timothy 4:7–8). Exercise is not a favourite pastime of many, as it is often hard work and takes time, commitment, and effort. Yet the benefits are better health and better living overall. Paul likens the need for exercise in godliness to natural exercise and the benefits it brings in this life and the one to come. Paul continues to instruct Timothy upon the focus of exercising one's self in godliness by explaining that it must be done in God's Word.

In 1 Timothy 4:12–16, Paul points out the following aspects regarding the exercises in godliness that all believers should commit to:
1) Set and be a good example for others.
2) Pay attention to reading the Word, exhortation, and doctrine.
3) Use your abilities and opportunities for good.

Godliness: Seeking to Please God

4) Direct your energy and strength on these, and your progress will be evident to all.

Paul writes to Timothy about the benefits of living life in pursuit of godliness and the power of God that is available when a person lives and devotes himself to such a high calling. However, Paul warns in 1 Timothy 6:3–10 about things the young man must avoid, refrain, and withdraw from:
1) Disputes and arguments over words.
2) Men who tussle over words.
3) Materialism and the love of money.

Paul's charge to Timothy concludes with the following reminder: *"But you, man of God, flee from all this, and pursue righteousness, godliness, faith, love, endurance and gentleness"* (1 Timothy 6:11, NIV). Thus, we learn that while abstaining from such things, we are also pursuing godliness.

EVIDENT TO ALL

We learn from Paul's letter to Timothy that our sole motivation for maintaining and operating in a pious conduct should be to please God. Godliness working on the grace team, added to faith (which pleases God), draws on the qualities of all the other team members, harnessing them for the ultimate purpose of pleasing God.

Pleasing and glorifying God is the bona fide display of living a pious life. That is where the power of God lies. It is released through godliness to the rest of the team already at work to grow us in the knowledge of Jesus Christ (2 Peter 1:5–8). Godliness magnifies the qualities of each grace, raising us to another degree in Christ and flooding earth's realm with glories from Heaven that have too long been denied. Earth has pined for the manifestations of the sons of the Most High. Romans 8:19 confirms the deep passion of creation regarding God's people: *"For the earnest expectation of the creature waiteth for the manifestation of the sons of God."*

Oh, what a destiny awaits! Much depends upon our quest to grow in the knowledge of Christ Jesus. God has not left us alone to accomplish such a glorious task. He has empowered us with all that pertains to life and godliness (2 Peter 1:3), thereby enabling us to be "can-do" people (Philippians 4:13). The Holy Spirit is leading us as God's children (Romans 8:14) into the full stature of Christ (Ephesians 4:13). With God's assistance, through His Word, His Blood, and His Spirit (1 John 5:7-8), as well as His glorious church and the members thereof, how can we fail? For with God, all things are possible. Thus living a godly life to its full potential is just a step of faith forward into God's "PLUS" realm. Our conduct, then, is sanctified for His glory. Our life of faith behaves more like God as we continue to grow in the knowledge of Christ, diligently adding to our faith the pluses Peter reveals: faith "PLUS" virtue "PLUS" knowledge "PLUS" temperance "PLUS" patience "PLUS" godliness… and still there is much more "PLUS" to come.

BROTHERLY Kindness: Loving the Brethren
chapter ten

In 1970, American singer Glen Campbell released a song on his sixteenth album entitled "Try a Little Kindness." The song encourages people to look beyond themselves to see the needs of others and then to lend a helping hand in order to make their lives a bit easier (see Jesus' teaching on the beatitudes in Matthew 6–7). The song's chorus summarizes the plea to humanity in this way:

> You've got to try a little kindness, just show a little kindness
> Shine your light for everyone to see
> And if you try a little kindness, you'll overlook the blindness
> Of the narrow-minded people on the narrow-minded streets[57]

---

[57] Austin, Bobby & Curt Sapaugh. "Try a Little Kindness." The Very Best of Glen Campbell. Capitol, 1970.

Michael C. Diotte

The world craves kindness, and from the words in this song, even "a little" would be well-appreciated. God has heard the cry of man's heart. In response, He has dispatched a living epistle (letter) to the church. It is a breathing communiqué written in the blood of His own Son, Jesus Christ, heralded over the globe for these past few thousand years. The church, Heaven's beacon, grows brighter and brighter even as the day approaches for her King's return, so that mankind may yet find her way to that which she hopes for—real, lasting kindness.

The church is mandated to reveal the effulgence of God's glory—the exact image, likeness, and form of Christ. Our growth in Christ is therefore pertinent to the fulfillment of this charge. Peter's passion is that we grow, expand, develop, and increase in this knowledge—beginning with faith. Moreover, we are to build upon faith, adding, harmonizing, and augmenting it with virtue, knowledge, temperance, patience, and godliness. As we do, Peter draws our focus to another addition in our developing process in Christ, as found in 2 Peter 1:5–7—brotherly kindness, an outward focus and demonstration toward others empowered by grace.

Brotherly kindness shapes our focus and behaviour toward others in the body as well as the sea of humanity. It is authorized to release the floodgates of man's newborn spirit, now dwelling in the earth on Christ's behalf, to unload a deluge of brotherly kindness upon humanity like never before. We are to give to the earth not just "a little" kindness, as many have pined for, but so much more than ever before. God has never held back what Heaven has, including His own Son (Romans 8:32). Thus, from the point of the cross, all things now are freely given. The church is God's beacon and distribution center for all that is freely given. We are not a reservoir, but a free flowing stream from Heaven's throne to water the dry and thirsty souls of humanity all over the world.

TWO YET ONE

Although two separate words—"brotherly" and "kindness"—they are united as one for a singular and powerful purpose. Brotherly kindness extends from the Greek word for *Philadelphia*, which is itself a combination of two words—*phileo* and *adelphos*. *Phileo* translates as

Brotherly Kindness: Loving the Brethren

"love" and *adelphos* means "brother." Merged together, it literally means "the love of brothers."

It is important for us to grasp this concept. A world of living, breathing people yet who are spiritually dead are watching the spiritually and fully alive "new man" in Christ (2 Corinthians 5:17), evaluating and concluding whether what we have is really what they need and want. What a marvellous opportunity is afforded the church to display openly just how good God is. Truly, the church is the most exciting place to be.

God has planned all along to reveal Himself to the world in the church—the body of Christ—*"the fulness of him that filleth all in all"* (Ephesians 1:23). Brotherly kindness in the church is not an optional grace to employ when or if a member in the body feels inspired, enlightened, or motivated to do so. It is an expectation God maintains for the entire body—all the members of Christ—period. Hebrews 13:1 plainly states, *"Let brotherly love continue."* We are not to allow any hindrances; brotherly love (kindness) must complete its assignment. As stewards of the *"manifold grace of God"* (1 Peter 4:10), we are to be found faithful (1 Corinthians 4:2) and ensure that all God expects and requires is carried out here upon the earth—even as it is in Heaven (Matthew 6:10).

In his writings to the Thessalonians, Paul stated that he didn't need to remind them to flow in brotherly kindness. His purpose was that they didn't stop there, however, but that they *"increase more and more"* (1 Thessalonians 4:10). Peter reveals that our walk in and obedience to the Word of God actually purifies our souls, and that through the Spirit (Spirit-led and Spirit-controlled life) we have unfeigned (real, sincere, genuine, authentic, truthful, honest, and heartfelt) love of the brethren. Notice that both obeying the truth and expressing love for one another is done through the Spirit. Living a true Spirit-led, Spirit-controlled life involves obedience to the Word and loving God's people.

We cannot claim to be "Word" people and "Holy Ghost" people if we do not have these two principles at work in our lives. Religion may think it is okay. Your own "self" may think, *Hey, it's not so bad. I'm doing pretty good,* but at the end of the day what really matters is what God thinks. With God, human reasoning doesn't wash. Suffice it to say that we are purified in order that we may love one another in the body of Christ through the Spirit.

Paul reminds us in Romans 12:10 to *"be kindly affected one to another with brotherly love; in honour preferring one another."* Brotherly kindness enables us to have or possess the ability to be kind, showing godly affection toward one another. Our treatment of one another is on display for the world to see. Man's response to the gospel message is largely dependent upon the church's daily behaviour and lifestyle. We are more directly responsible, through our behaviour and actions, for the salvation of souls than we realize.

Scripture spends a great deal of time, effort, and manpower to get these points across to God's people.

1) *There should be no schism in the body* (1 Corinthians 12:25).
2) *We are to prefer one another* (Romans 12:10).
3) *We are to put away lying, anger, stealing, laziness, greed, bitterness, corrupt communication, and evil speaking* (Ephesians 4:25–31).

Paul puts it succinctly in Ephesians 4:32—*"And be ye kind one to another, tenderhearted, forgiving one another, even as God for Christ's sake hath forgiven you."*

The mandate is clear— we are to go and preach this gospel (Mark 16:15). Preaching doesn't merely involve speaking words; God expects us to live what we are commissioned to preach. 2Corinthians 3:2 says, *"Ye are our epistle written in our hearts, known and read of all men."* God's view of His church on this earth is that we are living epistles (letters), sent and commissioned from Heaven to the earth for men and women everywhere to clearly read and intimately know God—as well as His love and passion for them!

We must not fail in demonstrating brotherly kindness to each other in the body of Christ, no matter what the situation or circumstance. The world is watching as the church continues to grow in the knowledge of Christ. It is not perfection we are attaining (that has already happened in

Brotherly Kindness: Loving the Brethren

Christ), but rather it is maturity in Christ we are seeking to display while stationed here on earth. In light of eternity, mankind's natural life is quite brief. The clearer and brighter our reflection of the King of kings and Lord of lords is, the more likely it is that fallen man will choose Jesus.

Brotherly kindness reveals to the world a true impression of God's family. Our association and interaction with each other in the body of Christ—no matter what earthly label we choose to identify ourselves with—is vital to the gospel message, for it shows what our Heavenly Father is all about and Who He really is.

BROTHERLY KINDNESS— *"DE RIGUEUR"*

The word *de rigueur* means "strictly required by the current fashion or by etiquette."[58] Heaven has etiquette, a custom or protocol that it follows. Unlike any other people or place here on the earth, Heaven's etiquette is of the highest integrity and purest motivation. Thus, all of Heaven's citizens conduct themselves by the same standards, customs, and protocols. It is Who God is; therefore, all He has made is of the same quality. Heaven's language is faith, its behaviour is love, and its current fashion (which is never outdated or in need of revision) is glory.

In our pursuit to grow in the knowledge of Christ, brotherly kindness is compulsory for knowing God.

> *Beloved, let us love one another: for love is of God; and every one that loveth is born of God, and knoweth God. He that loveth not knoweth not God; for God is love… If a man say, I love God, and hateth his brother, he is a liar: for he that loveth not his brother whom he hath seen, how can he love God whom he hath not seen? And this commandment have we from him, that he who loveth God love his brother also.* (1 John 4:7–8, 20–21)

For the one who truly desires to know God and grow in Christ, developing brotherly kindness is essential.

---

[58] Encarta World English Dictionary. "De rigueur." Accessed: April 2009 (http://encarta.msn.com/encnet/features/dictionary/DictionaryResults.aspx?lextype=3&search=de%20rigueur).

Jesus set this standard for His followers, clearly declaring in John 13:35 that the world will know who truly is a disciple of Christ *"if ye have love one to another."* This standard was not implemented to discourage us, but rather to keep us focused, assisting us in discerning the counterfeit from the genuine. Today, a lot is going on in the Name of God that has nothing to do with God. Following the teachings of Jesus found in the Word will steer us clear of that which is phony and set us toward that which is indisputably authentic and true.

In a world and society inundated with all manner of evil and darkness, God has commissioned the church to be a direct contrast. He has launched us into darkness, empowering us to shine before mankind (Matthew 5:16) so that they may see the good works and thus glorify our Father in Heaven. People need to see light, see good works, and thus see God. The church is the "sent one" to testify of and glorify God, so that living hope is once again inspired in the hearts of men. As the church demonstrates God's love in action toward one another, the peoples of the earth can view firsthand what Heaven is like. Brotherly kindness diligently employed in our daily lives will ensure that we portray a clear message before those who are desperate to be free. The church will fulfill Jesus' prayer for oneness and maturity with each other, as found in John 17:20–23. The saints would do well to memorize the cry of Jesus' heart, as recorded in His prayer in Gethsemane. It is our driving force!

As we grow in the knowledge of Christ, unity in the body is possible and maintained because of the cross. Keeping the cross in sight, we find the strength and ability to maturely work together, *"endeavouring to keep the unity of the Spirit in the bond of peace"* (Ephesians 4:3). To fulfill this aspect of scripture, it is key to first follow through with Ephesians 4:2, *"forbearing one another in love."* Developing and employing brotherly kindness in our daily lives with the members of the body of Christ will come with some intense moments, to put it mildly. However, as we stay committed to forbearing, being patient, long-suffering, forgiving, and merciful with one another, the rough edges in all our lives will become smoother and the image of Christ will shine more and more.

Operating in brotherly kindness requires the assistance of patience (cheerful endurance), as well as forgiveness and understanding. The

Brotherly Kindness: Loving the Brethren

believer must always do their best to keep in the forefront of their mind the principle mission according to 2 Corinthians 5:17–21, which is the ministry of reconciliation. As God's people, we are to reconcile everything—yes, *everything*—to God. This includes each other and should be done in the spirit of brotherly kindness. Brotherly kindness allows time for repentance and reconciliation so that unity and oneness in Christ may be maintained, as well as the mission of the church fulfilled. Lack of brotherly kindness has fragmented and driven us apart on a global scale. Fallen man looks on in despair and even greater fear, for the church was its only hope for everlasting life.

RECIPE FOR BROTHERLY KINDNESS

The Word of God holds for us the key to success in every area of life. Being kind to one another can and will become a natural thing as we are diligent to cultivate the soil of our hearts and minds, allowing God to sow and grow the incorruptible seed of His Word (1 Peter 1:22–23) in our lives to manifest the express image of His Son Jesus. Romans 8:29 reminds us that God's sole objective is to conform us into the image of His Son Jesus.

The following points will assist us in remembering what is called for when believers walk in and demonstrate brotherly kindness.

1) Our souls (mind, will, emotions, and intellect) must be purified (1 Peter 1:21–22). This is done through obedience to the Word of God. Thus, sincere and fervent love of the brethren is easily obtainable.

2) We need to be students of the Word, to be taught of God and those He has given to equip us, as seen in 1 Thessalonians 4:9–10 and Ephesians 4:8–16. God Himself teaches us the meaning of love in 1 John 4:9–10, and demonstrates openly His love toward us through the sacrifice of His own Son (1 John 3:16). Meditating upon the demonstration of God's love toward us in Jesus will help us move into the operation of brotherly kindness more easily.

3) Brotherly kindness entails that we spend more time corporately with one another. Too many Christians

today are afraid of getting involved with each other. Past experiences have caused them to hesitate and protect themselves from further disappointments and pain. If God took this approach, man would still yet be lost in his sin.

Scripture reminds us in Romans 5:8 that *"while we were yet sinners, Christ died for us."* God knows that pain of reaching out to those who are lost, fearful, untrusting, and hateful, yet He Himself did not hold back. Thus, He expects us to do the same. As He gave of Himself to win us, so we likewise must give of ourselves in His Name to others.

As frightening and overwhelming as it can become when spending time with the brethren, if we'll go through the process we will learn and understand what real ministry to the body is like and how rewarding it can be. Yes, there will be disappointments, and perhaps even hurts, but it does not validate our philosophy that it is better to withdraw and minister at a distance. God's Word teaches no such philosophy, nor does it validate isolation from His body and its members, no matter what state it is in.

As we each are faithful to look to Him (Hebrews 12:1–2), drawing our strength from Him directly, as well as drawing daily our refreshing from our communion with the Holy Spirit, we will remain strong and readied to supply edification and exhortation to every member, every day (Ephesians 4:16, Hebrews 3:13). As we forget ourselves and live totally for Him, we can't help but fall in love with the brethren and give our lives to them, for in doing so we are truly loving Christ and His body and giving our lives for Him.

Brotherly kindness also requires us to pray for each other in the body of Christ. Ephesians 6:18 reminds us that prayer, supplication, and watching with all perseverance and supplication is *"for all saints."* Our personal clashes must not be allowed to deter us from praying fervently for each other. Remember the command in Hebrews 13:1—*"Let brotherly love continue."* Nothing must stand in the way of brotherly love—not our own feelings, hurts, or fears. James, the half-brother of Jesus, shows us brotherly kindness in action in James 5:16. Brotherly love includes confessing our faults (literally our slips, lapses, or deviations) as well

Brotherly Kindness: Loving the Brethren

as now employing prayer for one another so that we may be healed (restored).

FOR ALL TO SEE

Concerning brotherly kindness, James summarized it well. In short, it must be acted upon as well as demonstrated for others to see. It is to be a living witness to the world that faith in God and living for Him is worth the effort. The world will see the Word of God in full demonstration by how we treat one another. Paul lays it out for us in Romans 15:1—*"We then that are strong ought to bear the infirmities of the weak, and not to please ourselves."* The more we mature and grow in Christ, the more is expected of us to help others who are growing and developing. As we strengthen and treat our own brothers well, considering and preferring them, the world will see and learn how the family and kingdom of God operates.

Sometimes in a family, stuff happens. When it does, although the family may experience disruption and hard times, they come together to work it out. As they take this approach in a loving way, they are strengthened and experience a stronger bond to hold them in the future. It is much the same in the body of Christ, the family of God. Sometimes various members find themselves in a struggle to overcome some habit, test, trial, or tribulation. As we mature in Christ, we remember that we too have been through some tough moments and have had to grow through difficult times. Thus, our attitude toward our family in Christ is not to offend (1 Corinthians 8:13), but to serve each other (Galatians 5:13). This is to the benefit of ourselves, the overall body of Christ, and the watching world.

The grace of brotherly kindness at work in our lives and in the church will cause us each to be wise in our treatment of each other (James 4:11–12). Our focus toward each other is never done through judgment or criticism. Much of what the modern church claims to be constructive criticism is just plain destructive. We only need look at the end result upon our brother to know this to be true. John 3:17 is clear—Jesus didn't come to condemn but to administer life to others. As His body, His church, and His representatives here in the earth, we possess the same goal and mandate. Jesus never walked around treating His followers in the manner many in the church do to one another today.

Paul explains in 1 Thessalonians 5:14 about our mature conduct toward one another and what it is to be. We notice that he uses the word "warn." This word comes from the Greek word *noutheteo*, meaning "to put in mind, to caution or reprove gently."[59] Immediately we catch the spirit, attitude, and tone of Paul's choice of words here. Brotherly kindness is not harsh, demeaning, or condescending in its tone or word to another saint. Rather, we are to reprove cautiously and gently, keeping in mind to whom we are speaking and the end result we wish to obtain—which is always to glorify God. Living in this world is difficult enough; we don't need our own brethren coming down hard on us so as to break us and leave us in a worse state than when they found us.

As we mature and grow in the knowledge of Christ Jesus, we will find ourselves comforting and upholding others, as Paul instructed in 1 Thessalonians 5:14, as well as being patient (cheerfully enduring) with the brethren. Our pursuit with regards to one another is to follow after those things that make for peace and that edify (Romans 14:19). When leaving our presence, for the most part people should leave in a better state than when we first happened upon them. Our deposit into another person's life should be that of faith, hope, and love woven tightly with encouragement, exhortation, and edification.

Brotherly kindness works with the rest of the grace team to ensure that our effect upon our own family of God is an inspiration to the watching world, thus clearly demonstrating to them what their own lives can and will be like if they will make Jesus their Lord and join the family of God. To the degree we develop a strong love and appreciation for the body of Christ and the church of the living God, we will display the love of Christ to them, thereby persuading them one way or the other whether the glorious gospel we represent is for them.

As we increase more and more in our open affection for each other in the church, our faith will multiply exponentially. The other

---

[59] Strong, James. *Strong's Exhaustive Concordance of the Bible* (Iowa Falls, IA: Riverside Book and Bible House, 1992), p. 50. See #3560.

Brotherly Kindness: Loving the Brethren

members of the grace team—virtue, knowledge, temperance, patience, and godliness—will ignite us to new levels in Christ, empowering our faith to multiply and increase even more. The world will begin to stand and take notice of the church and the Lord of the church. The fear of the Lord will come upon every soul (Acts 2:42–47) as the culture of the kingdom of our Lord and Christ begins to flow freely from the church of the living God. Men everywhere will begin to say one to another:

Come ye, and let us go up to the mountain of the Lord... he will teach us of his ways, and we will walk in his paths: for out of Zion shall go forth the law, and the word of the Lord from Jerusalem. (Isaiah 2:3)

Paul declares in 1 Thessalonians 3:12, *"And the Lord make you to increase and abound in love one to another, and toward all men, even as we do toward you."* Increase is God's plan and design. Peter makes sure to strategically place each of the graces in a specific order so that our growth is methodical, prosperous, and a glory to God. God is glorified when we add to our faith virtue "PLUS" knowledge "PLUS" temperance "PLUS" patience "PLUS" godliness "PLUS" brotherly kindness. All of these added diligently into our lives bring us into a fuller and more exact image and likeness of Christ for the world to see. Yet, there is more! This next addition will complete the team, taking us into a place of comprehension in Christ that surpasses knowledge (Ephesians 3:16–21). The greatest "PLUS" is…

CHARITY: *Generous Love*
chapter eleven

One thing that makes charity (*agape*, the God-kind of love) so great is its ability to be generous despite how negative, dark, or evil a situation may be. Kenneth Copeland says:

> In this world where nothing is failure-proof, we have been given complete access to God's love. Love is the cardinal law of God—it never fails. Put the love of God into operation and you will succeed (1 Corinthians 13:8).[60]

Peter does not finalize his steps to growing in the knowledge of Christ until he comes to charity. Growth in the knowledge of Christ Jesus necessitates the maturing of Christ-like character in our lives. We are reminded in Peter's correspondence to the saints that such maturity

---

[60] Copeland, Kenneth. *Walking in the Realm of the Miraculous* (Fort Worth, TX: Kenneth Copeland Publications, 1979), p. 15.

involves our employing diligence as we add the various graces to our faith. As we merge this team of eight graces together, our growth will become apparent to all and bring glory to our Heavenly Father. The measure of faith we received from God is complemented by the graces that follow it—virtue, knowledge, temperance, perseverance, godliness, brotherly kindness, and charity.

Again, our goal according to 2 Peter 1:5–8 is to grow in the knowledge of Christ. Paul reminds us in Romans 8:29 that God's focus for our lives in Christ is that we be conformed to the image of His Son. Manifesting the character and nature of Jesus in our lives is no small undertaking. As we receive, employ, and work each of the qualities Peter mentions, each dimension (grace) will fit into and develop the others. Together they will become a formidable team.

Charity embodies the grace team and epitomizes the work they do while also characterizing their mission and objective in a believer's life. Scripture places high priority upon charity and reveals God's thoughts about its importance in our lives as Christians. 1 Corinthians 13:13 teaches that charity is the greatest, among faith and hope. In his writings, Paul gives preeminence to charity out of all the nine fruit of the spirit (Galatians 5:22). In Colossians 3:14, Paul emphasizes charity's role: *"And above all these things put on charity, which is the bond of perfectness."* Charity—or love, as we have come to say—is different than brotherly kindness.

AGAPE'S MOTTO: OTHERS

The New Testament speaks of four different types of love. Modern society, in general, often uses one word to cover the entire spectrum of human friendship, dating, family, and intimacy: "love." We'll even use the term in regards to our favourite foods ("I love this meal") or clothing ("I love that outfit"). Our use of the term "love" in this manner has affected our ability to know and understand what true love really is. Perhaps as we grow to properly understand the various terms, employing them in our daily understanding and vocabulary, misconceptions and misunderstandings about love will be cleared up. Thus, we'll enjoy a more effective love walk on all levels.

There are four words used in the New Testament to define the various aspects of love. The New Testament was written in common Greek, hence the four words are:
1) *Philia*, which is the love of close friends or brothers.
2) *Storge*, which is the love of one's family.
3) *Eros*, which is sexual or carnal love.
4) *Agape*, which is the God-kind of love, that love which seeks the highest good of others. *Agape* does not base the release of its love on another person's merits or achievements.

Author and minister Marilyn Hickey writes:

The fourth kind of love is *agape* love. This is the kind of love that gives and doesn't expect anything in return. It has no strings attached. It is the God-kind of love, the kind of love that God displayed when He so loved the world that He gave His only begotten Son (John 3:16)… He loves us even if we don't love Him back. That's unconditional love![61]

Jesus explains in Matthew 5:44, *"But I say unto you, Love your enemies, bless them that curse you, do good to them that hate you, and pray for them which despitefully use you, and persecute you."* We see that charity surpasses brotherly kindness; charity goes beyond love of its own.

Charity encompasses humanity around the globe. It is an all-embracing benevolence purposely released toward those in need. What is mankind's need? To know real charity. Charity is a concentrated exercise of the will. Remember John 3:16? *"For God so loved the world, that he gave…"* Understand that charity is not the kind of love that waits for others to perform correctly or to obtain some predetermined standard. Nor does charity stand at a distance, picking first whom it becomes involved with. Absolutely not! If God operated under that *modus operandi*, He probably would never again have involved Himself

---

[61] Hickey, Marilyn. *God's Covenant for Your Family* (Tulsa, OK: Harrison House, 1982), p. 97.

Charity: Generous Love

in the affairs of the human race and would still be waiting for man to meet certain standards before sending Jesus. By now, we may be thinking, *That's absurd. God wouldn't operate like that.* Christian, believer, we are born of Him. We live, move, and have our very being in Him (Acts 17:28). Thus, now we live by the same standard and principles He does.

Whether we fully comprehend it or not, being born again of His Spirit—having become citizens of His realm, wearing His Name, calling Him Saviour, Master, and Lord—obligates us to live by the same standards and principles God Himself lives by—which is love.

Kenneth Copeland remarked:

> It is a must that you learn how to operate in God's love. To do that requires faith. You have to develop your faith in His love to the point that it governs your thinking, your speech, and your actions. You must have your mind so renewed that you function entirely according to God's love rather than the methods and systems of the world.[62]

Bible Teacher and bestselling author Joyce Meyer states:

> As children of God, we must love others as God loves us. Love is an effort. We will never love anybody if we are not willing to pay the price.[63]

Walking in love now becomes our pursuit. Hence, come what may, we are dedicated to the well-being and active goodwill of others. Regarding our display of love toward others, Marilyn Hickey says:

> If you are waiting for an emotion, you will never experience God's love. You experience God's love when you love by faith.

---

[62] Copeland, Kenneth. *Walking in the Realm of the Miraculous* (Fort Worth, TX: Kenneth Copeland Publications, 1979), p. 15.
[63] Meyer, Joyce. *Straight Talk on Discouragement* (Brentwood, TN: Warner Faith Publishing, 1998), p. 28.

Michael C. Diotte

Paul says in Colossians 3:14 that we are to put on love. You put it on by faith.[64]

Musicians and songwriters Charles D. Meig and Elizabeth M. Shields penned the following words that well describe the motto of charity:

Verse 1: Lord, help me to live from day to day
In such a self-forgetful way
That even when I kneel to pray
My prayer shall be for—others
Verse 2: Help me in all the work I do
To ever be sincere and true
And know that all I'd do for You
Must needs be done for—others
Chorus: Others, Lord, yes, others
Let this my motto be
Help me to live for others
That I may live like Thee!
Verse 3: Let "self" be crucified and slain
And buried deep; and all in vain
May efforts be to rise again
Unless to live for—others
Verse 4: And when my work on earth is done
And my new work in heaven's begun
May I forget the crown I've won
While thinking still of—others[65]

GOD'S EXAMPLE

God Himself sets no different standard. What He expects of His people, the body of Christ, He expects of Himself, adhering to charity's tenets. Because He is also the God of love, He empowers us with His love so that we are able to rise to meet the demands of love. Romans 5:8 shows God's love in action: while we were still yet sinners (undesirables),

---

[64] Hickey, Marilyn. *God's Covenant for Your Family* (City, State/Province: Harrison House, 1982), p. 102.
[65] Meig, Charles D. & Elizabeth M. Shields. "Others." 1917.

Christ still came and died for us. His action toward us was love motivated. He didn't wait for us to change before getting involved; love moved Him to get involved despite our sin-filled, fallen state. He lived out charity right before our very eyes and showed us a better way. Ephesians 2:4–7 describes this fascinating and passionate move of love and calls it *"his great love."*

Jesus, God's Son, follows the pattern set by His Father and comes into the darkness of mankind's societal state. 1 John 3:16 says, *"This is how we know what love is: Jesus Christ laid down his life for us. And we ought to lay down our lives for our brothers"* (NIV). John 15:13 says that this type of love is the greatest love there is: *"Greater love has no one than this, that he lay down his life for his friends"* (NIV). We see that our Heavenly Father, as well as our Lord and Saviour Jesus, has openly demonstrated charity for us. We now have a model to build and act upon with regards to our interactions and relationship building. Active goodwill toward others is no longer a surprise, but our motto.

A MORE EXCELLENT WAY

Previously, we saw in Matthew 5:43–44 Jesus' command to love even our enemies. When we walk in love—we walk in a more excellent way.

> *But earnestly desire and zealously cultivate the greatest and best gifts and graces (the higher gifts and the choicest graces). And yet I will show you a still more excellent way [one that is better by far and the highest of them all—love].* (1 Corinthians 12:3, AMP)

Love (charity) is the main thing for every believer to focus on. It is a more excellent way, and the Amplified Bible records for us that love is *"better by far and the highest of them all."*

Continuing His teaching in Matthew 5, Jesus reveals His expectation that we love even our enemies, so that we *"may be the children of your Father which is in heaven"* (Matthew 5:45). Jesus endeavours to take us further, beyond the realm of brotherly kindness, because even sinners can love each other (Matthew 5:46–47). As a different breed of people—a heavenly class, chosen, royal, and peculiar (1 Peter 2:9)—like our Heavenly Father, much more is expected of us.

> *You, therefore, must be perfect [growing into complete maturity of godliness in mind and character, having reached the proper height of virtue and integrity], as your heavenly Father is perfect.* (Matthew 5:48, AMP)

Luke 6:35–36 reinforces the teaching of Matthew 5:48 and brings to our understanding that this is the standard of God for all His followers, the principle by which Heaven operates. The conclusion, then, as we grow in the knowledge of Christ, is clear when it comes to our actions and behaviours toward anyone other than ourselves. We must demonstrate active good will toward all. Just as God was toward us, so we need to be toward everyone on the planet. We are now Heaven's ambassadors (2 Corinthians 5:17–21) and our ministry is a global one to nations.

LOVE'S PERFORMANCE

Scripture shows love to be a necessary component to our Christian lives. Authors James MacDonald and Barb Peil comment on love:

> Love is rooted in God's character. His conduct flows out of His character because God is love, because God loves. A commitment to loving God will send ripple effects to your other relationships. The closer you walk with God, the more His Spirit will give you the power to love others as God loves them.[66]

The following passages from the New Testament provide further insight into love's role in our lives. Ephesians 5:2 says we are to *"walk in love."* Colossians 3:14 reminds us to *"put on charity [love]."* 1 Corinthians 16:14 tells us to *"do everything in love"* (NIV). Colossians 2:2 echoes this sentiment, that we should be *"knit together in love."* Galatians 5:13

---

[66] MacDonald, James & Barb Peil. *Lord, Change My Attitude* (Chicago, IL: Lifeway Press, 2008), p. 108.

speaks to our service—*"by love serve one another."* Each passage gives testimony to our conduct toward others and the components needed to live the Christian life effectively. The Word also addresses our Christian liberty. It speaks to every aspect of our living in, through, and for Christ, and also governs our actions so that love is demonstrated and revealed in everything we do, think, and say.

God is our governing force, for God is love (1 John 4:8). A.W. Tozer, author of the book *The Knowledge of the Holy*, comments:

> The words "God is love" mean that love is an essential attribute of God. Love is something true of God but it is not God. It expresses the way God is in His unitary being… He always acts like Himself, and because He is a unity He never suspends one of His attributes in order to exercise another.[67]

MATURED LOVE

Growing in love is really not difficult. Neither is growing in the knowledge of Christ Jesus (2 Peter 1:5–7). It takes faith. Simply put, it means taking the faith we received at the new birth and diligently employing it. Luke 11:34 says, *"The light of the body is the eye: therefore when thine eye is single, thy whole body also is full of light; but when thine eye is evil, thy body also is full of darkness."* Our focus as we develop often determines the ease of the lessons we learn. Far too many Christians have their eyes on more than they can process. Perhaps this is a result of the current world system's influence in their lives.

It's hectic out there. The world doesn't know whether it is coming or going. It'll load you up with its philosophies, issues, and important matters so quick that you'll feel like you're living in an overwhelmed state 24/7. The world's overwhelmed living is not what we need. God does want us to be overwhelmed, but with His blessing, His life, and His love. So let's keep our eyes focused on Jesus (Hebrews 12:1–2). Set them so that they have a singular focus and you'll be full of light. Thus, our

---

[67] Tozer, A.W. *The Knowledge of the Holy* (New York, NY: Harper & Row Publishers, 1961), p. 105.

growth in Christ and all the facets of His grace will actually become much easier, for there will be no darkness or confusion but rather peace.

God Himself will also be our instructor, as Paul reminds us in 1 Thessalonians 4:9–10. He teaches by the very goodness of His character, which is love (1 John 4:8). Exodus 34:6–7 explains that God's character includes grace, mercy, long-suffering, and abundant goodness. We learn to grow in love by God's own example. Both 1 John 4:9 and Romans 5:8 reveal God's love in action toward us—that even while we were still in our sin He sent His Son, Jesus, to die on our behalf. 1 John 4:10 further expounds on God's demonstration of His love toward us by stating, *"Herein is love, not that we loved God, but that he loved us, and sent his Son to be the propitiation for our sins."* The Apostle John then continues in the next verse to show us that what we see God do, we now must do toward one another—*"Beloved, if God so loved us, we ought also to love one another"* (1 John 4:11).

Jesus also teaches us through His life examples and teachings to grow and mature in charity (love). 1 John 3:16 explains how we will know real love—or *agape*, the God-kind of love. We identify it by its ability to lay down its life for another. In Ephesians 5:2, we learn that we are to walk in love the same way Christ walked in love. Whatever He does, we must do the same. Jesus was specific on the matter of us growing in love toward others. He said, *"Love one another; as I have loved you"* (John 13:34). As Christians, the more time we spend meditating upon how Jesus lived, died, and rose again, the more we'll comprehend the true meaning of charity, which is love.

The Apostle Paul, in his writings, also elaborates for the church about growing and maturing in love. Paul's dissertation, found in 1 Corinthians 13:4–8, describes love in action. He writes about his passion for us to grow in love and its ways. 1 Thessalonians 3:12 says, *"And the Lord make you to increase and abound in love one toward another, and toward all men, even as we do toward you."* Increase, is on Paul's heart and mind—increase in demonstrated love (charity) toward others.

Both Ephesians 3:17–19 and Philippians 1:9 disclose for us additional aspects to increasing in love. Paul recaps and streamlines for us the need to increase in love, but also to be rooted and grounded in it through knowledge and judgment. Growth in love is desired, anticipated, and expected. Demonstrating love toward mankind (active good will toward all) is the next step. Jesus commanded us to *"go ye into all the world, and preach..."* (Mark 16:15). God's love demonstrated toward humanity is the Word revealed (John 1:14) and the Word proclaimed (Romans 10:8). There lies our task as Christ-like ones: proclaim and demonstrate Christ by manifesting love... for God *is* love and this love is shed abroad in our hearts by the Holy Ghost (Romans 5:5).

THE UNVEILING
In her book, *God's Will for You*, Bible teacher and author Gloria Copeland states:

> God is love and you have been recreated in the image of Him. Your new nature is agape love. You are the love of God... The world is starved for love. God made man to receive love. The deepest yearning of every man is to be loved and cared for—a desire that can only be fulfilled through the love of God.[68]

John 3:16's message is indelibly written upon the hearts and minds of so many: *"For God so loved the world..."* The world's artists and musicians have embodied man's unceasing desire for real love. The words penned in this simple song from 1965 give us a glimpse into this desire:

> What the world needs now is love, sweet love.
> It's the only thing that there's just too little of.
> What the world needs now is love, sweet love,
> No not just for some, but for everyone.[69]

Humanity continues to imagine what love is and what it really is like. The theme of perfected love weaves throughout mankind's culture,

---

[68] Copeland, Gloria. *God's Will for You* (Fort Worth, TX: Kenneth Copeland Publications, 1972), pp. 88–89.
[69] David, Hal & Burt Bacharach. "What the World Needs Now Is Love." What the World Needs Now Is Love. Imperial Records, 1965.

being expressed and seen on every societal level. The church is privileged to be the carriers and demonstrators of the very perfected love that the world desires and pines for.

As we follow the direction in the Word for "unveiling" perfected love, the world will begin to behold with their own eyes God's heart for them, seeing *"what manner of love the Father hath bestowed upon us"* (1 John 3:1), calling us sons. To accomplish such an unveiling to the world, God's Word provides us with the means to successfully obtain His directive. John 14:15 instructs us to obey what He commands. John 14:21 clarifies for us that having and obeying the Word is how we express our love for God (see also 1 John 5:3) and opens up the opportunity for God to further display His love for us openly so that the world may see and believe (John 17:21–23). In unveiling God's love, the world will also see the church actively loving each other, as shown in 1 John 4:20–21. Hatred and dislike for another saint is an unthinkable act for those who possess and obey the Word of God.

True faith in Christ automatically ushers us into the love realm of God (1 John 5:1). Faith working by love (Galatians 5:6) keeps us walking and abiding in victory. So as good stewards of the manifold grace of God (1 Peter 4:10), we monitor our own hearts, keeping them free of the world's debris by simply trusting and obeying the Word.

Mankind will gaze upon the church with amazement and awe, igniting the fear of the Lord in their lives, all because they see God's love manifesting before them by our simple obedience to His Word (1 John 5:2). This is how God's children behave and act in private (church life) and in public (before the world), as Jesus taught us in Matthew 5:43–48. As we see in 1 John 3:18, love is not about word and tongue but *"in deed and in truth."* Love is the better, more excellent way.

God's charity *agape* answers the longing of man's heart for real, perfected love. He has chosen the vehicle of the church to manifest love to the world. It's what the world needs now—"love, sweet love—no not just for some, but for everyone." The cross of Jesus personifies that love and remains to this day a beacon for whosoever will come (Mark 8:34). With charity now taking its place upon the grace team, our growth in the knowledge of Christ Jesus is accelerated.

Charity: Generous Love

We have come to understand that this growth requires effort on our part. Not some, but the giving of *all* diligence. We are encouraged to employ every effort to accomplish the task at hand—to be like Jesus right now, in the earth. Faith in Christ opens the door to becoming like Him in this life. The deposit we received into our hearts of the incorruptible seed of God's Word caused such a glorious transformation to take place that Paul could only describe it by using the phrase *"new creature"*—or, as another translation puts it, *"Therefore if any person is [ingrafted] in Christ (the Messiah) he is a new creation (a new creature altogether); the old [previous moral and spiritual condition] has passed away"* (2 Corinthians 5:17, AMP).

Faith is only the beginning—a step forward into God's realm of "PLUS". It is not just one more addition, but more than we could ever ask, imagine, or think. Faith in Christ, received at the cross of Christ, opens man to possibilities never before dreamed. Faith is partnered with a team of seven other graces which blend themselves together in harmony with faith—increasing faith's ability to overcome anything, remain victorious in everything, and accomplish the impossible. For with God, all things are possible. All you have to do is believe.

The realm of faith is expanded to faith "PLUS" virtue (excellence) "PLUS" knowledge (increasing knowledge of God) "PLUS" temperance (self-control) "PLUS" patience (cheerful endurance) "PLUS" godliness (reverence, piety) "PLUS" brotherly kindness (love of the brethren) "PLUS" charity (*agape*, the God-kind of love). These eight graces working together in our lives produce the character of Christ, opening us up to God's "PLUS" realm, where *"all things are become new"* (2 Corinthians 5:17). Eight is the number of new beginnings, and with these eight graces at work in an ever-increasing measure in our lives, we'll be forever changed (2 Corinthians 3:18).

Is it worth all the effort? Peter assures us it is by reminding us that grace and peace are multiplied in our lives (2 Peter 1:2). Everything pertaining to life and godliness are bestowed (2 Peter 1:3). Spiritual blindness and spiritual forgetfulness are avoided (2 Peter 1:9). We will not stumble or fall (2 Peter 1:10). And finally, we will be granted an abundant entrance into the everlasting kingdom of our God (2 Peter 1:11). Growth in Christ is worth it, and it is glorious… "PLUS" so much more!

WHAT'S *In You?*
chapter twelve

If we can understand and comprehend what is now in us, we can radically change and never live below our means in God another day. This book has endeavoured to focus its study upon the text of 2 Peter 1:5–7. We learned that faith does not stand alone, but has seven other associates added to it so that we may effectively grow in the knowledge of our Lord and Saviour Jesus Christ.

When an individual comes to the cross of Jesus Christ, receiving Him as their Saviour and Lord, faith is imparted. Romans 12:3 expresses, *"According as God hath dealt to every man the measure of faith."* Thus, we discover that God Himself has given us the measure of faith. Galatians 2:20, elaborates further that *"the life which I now live in the flesh I live by the faith of the Son of God."* The faith we have from God and live by is that of the Son of God. We are no longer faithless. Faith is *now* in us.

Paul's writing to the Colossians reveals something even more fabulous residing on the inside of us as Christians. Colossians 1:27 says,

What's In You?

"To whom God would make known what is the riches of the glory of this mystery among the Gentiles; which is Christ in you, the hope of glory." John 17:23 finds Jesus making a remarkable statement: *"I in them, and thou in me that they may be made perfect in one."* Inside every believer lives Christ Jesus. We are no longer alone. Christ Himself is *now* in us. Jesus' own words, found in John 14:23, say, *"If a man love me, he will keep my words: and my Father will love him, and we will come unto him, and make our abode with him."*

Speaker and author Charles Capps gives insight into what Jesus is saying in this verse:

> This is one of the great truths of the Scriptures. God the Father, the Son, and the Holy Ghost are in you. Loving God and keeping His Word creates the life style of God within you. And God will inhabit you in the fullness of the Godhead.[70]

Amazing! Think about it! We have inside of us Christ, the hope of glory, and His faith as well. The God-kind of faith is dwelling in us, along with God Himself. Now that is beyond the mind's ability to comprehend. Hence, the Christian needs faith to be able to understand all of these marvellous God-happenings (Hebrews 11:3). Colossians 2:9–10 teaches us that the fullness of the Godhead bodily dwells in Christ and that in Christ we are now complete. Christ dwelling in us then means that the Godhead bodily also dwells in us.

Consistent with God's character and nature, we discover that there is more. God's realm and kingdom is like that—filled with "PLUS". We hear additional information from God's Word about what is in us. For all to hear, 1 Corinthians 3:16 exclaims news that we must not miss: *"Know ye not that ye are the temple of God, and that the Spirit of God dwelleth in you?"* Now that Christ and His faith are in us—and we have been transformed to become new (2 Corinthians 5:17)—we see that the Holy Spirit also has come to live inside of us. It is important for us to spend time meditating and understanding.

---

[70] Capps, Charles. *God's Image of You* (Tulsa, OK: Harrison House, 1985), pp. 63–64

Michael C. Diotte

Our study has been about *Faith Plus*. God is all about putting more "PLUS" into our lives. The entire Godhead dwelling in Christ bodily, and then Christ dwelling in us, is evidence of this. As Christians, we were not designed in Christ to come behind in any good thing. We were designed in Christ's image and likeness.

Christ's own faith is now in us, along with all of its associates—virtue, knowledge, temperance, patience, godliness, brotherly kindness, and charity (2 Peter 1:5–7). How can we ever fail doing His will when empowered with so much? Ephesians 3:17 reminds us, *"Christ may dwell in your hearts by faith; that ye, being rooted and grounded in love."* Faith is the premise for Christ dwelling in us. He gives us His own faith—"the measure of faith," as we learned earlier—so that He could dwell in our hearts. That faith, which is given to us, operates and is energized by the love we are rooted and grounded in. Hence, it must be a high priority for every believer to become established firmly in the "love walk." The success of his or her faith depends on it.

God's Word reveals more about what is now in us. Ephesians 3:16 explains that strength is in our inner man (the reborn man in Christ). Not just any kind of strength, but God's strength, provided by His Spirit.

Ephesians 5:19 sings, *"Making melody in your heart to the Lord."* Your heart, that inner man which is new in Christ, has a tremendous capacity to receive more from God. With the fullness of the Godhead bodily dwelling in us through Christ, as well as Christ's own faith and all the seven associates of faith, along with strength provided by the Spirit and the melodies of psalms, hymns, and spiritual songs, we have been enlarged far beyond what we could have ever asked, imagined, or thought.

Philippians 2:5 bears news about the mind of Christ: *"Let this mind be in you, which was also in Christ Jesus."* We have His mind—we only need to allow it in us. Paul tells us in his writings that if we'll allow it to happen, the mind of Christ will rise up in us as well.

Paul continues to explain that *"the peace of God, which passeth all understanding, shall keep your hearts and minds through Christ Jesus"* (Philippians 4:7). God's peace is in us as well. He brings it with Him. His peace will keep our hearts and minds stable. They will be kept through Christ. Everything that God is—His fullness—is in us. As His children, we lack nothing. Anything that we need pertaining to life and godliness is available to us and is ours (2 Peter 1:3).

We should add one more thing before we move on. In Colossians 3:16, Paul specifically drew the believer's attention to this truth about what was in them: *"Let the word of Christ dwell in you richly in all wisdom."* Jesus spoke in John 15:7 concerning His Word and us: *"If ye abide in me, and my words abide in you, ye shall ask what ye will, and it shall be done unto you."* Living and abiding in His Word is the key to a stronger faith and its team of associates. God's Word is in us, ready to take us from faith to faith (Romans 1:17) and glory to glory (2 Corinthians 3:18). Faith and its complete grace team need the Word of God to accomplish its mission to grow us in the knowledge of Christ Jesus.

God's Word is there. We have free access to it, thus there is no need for any Christian (Christ-like one) to live any lower than Jesus revealed and demonstrated for us. We are now in Christ—John 15:7 reminds us that we abide in Christ. The only thing missing to have a dynamic Christian life unfold in our lives, as God has repeatedly promised in His Word, is for the saint of God to allow the Word of God to abide in them. Make the decision to give God's Word the highest priority in your life. In doing so, you'll provide your faith—"PLUS" virtue "PLUS" knowledge "PLUS" temperance "PLUS" patience "PLUS" godliness "PLUS" brotherly kindness "PLUS" charity—with the food and sustenance it needs to bring you into God's "PLUS" realm where all things are possible. Only believe. It'll be easy to believe, for you are now abiding, dwelling, and living in the Word of God richly.

With your faith feasting upon the rich abundance of God's Word, you will surely be rewarded with:
1) Grace and peace, multiplied through the knowledge of Christ.
2) All that pertains to life and godliness.
3) Glory and virtue.
4) Exceeding great and precious promises.

5) The ability to partake of the divine nature.
6) Escape from the corruption in the world.
7) Fruitfulness and abundance.
8) An abundant entrance into the everlasting kingdom of our Lord and Saviour Jesus Christ.

A new beginning awaits!

The Scripture encourages us, in Hebrews 10:23, to *"hold fast the profession of our faith without wavering."* The following is a profession of faith based upon our study of 2 Peter 1:5–7:

> Heavenly Father, for the very reason that Your Word declares, states, and teaches me to do so—not losing a minute in building upon what has been given to me—I add and join my diligence to Your divine promises, as a musical instrument is added to an orchestra and yields itself to the direction of the maestro. I employ every effort in exercising and complementing my faith to develop Christ's character of virtue (excellence, resolution and Christian energy, good character). In exercising virtue, I develop knowledge (intelligence, spiritual understanding), and in exercising knowledge, I develop self-control (temperance, alert discipline). In exercising self-control, I develop steadfastness (passionate patience, cheerful endurance), and in exercising steadfastness, I develop godliness (piety, reverent wonder). In exercising godliness, I develop brotherly affection (kindness, warm friendliness), and in exercising brotherly affection, I develop charity (*agape*, generous, Christ-like love).
>
> Father, I thank You that each of these qualities are actively working in me and fitting into and developing each of the other qualities so that my life reflects the full image and likeness of Christ, my Lord and Saviour. I thank You, Father, that these qualities are mine and are increasingly abounding in me. I am maturing daily in my relationship and experience of my Master Jesus. These Christ-like qualities abound in me and keep me from being idle or unfruitful unto the full personal knowledge

of my Lord Jesus Christ (the Messiah, the Anointed One). Their abundance in my life keeps me fruitful, and always abounding in the knowledge of Jesus Christ. Thank You, Father, that You are glorified in me through Jesus Christ, Your Son. In Jesus' Name, Amen!

Make this profession of faith from the scriptures a regular part of your prayer and devotion time. Allow your heart and mind time to meditate upon the truth Peter teaches, so that you may grow in the knowledge of Him, Christ Jesus your Lord and Saviour, Who gave Himself freely for you. Know what (and Who) is in you.

It never has been complicated to live the Christ-like life. You can do it, because you are a child of God (1 John 4:4). The Greater One (Jesus) lives inside of you to give you life more abundantly (John 10:10). It's a life full of God, faith, glory and so much more than ever before. It's a life full of faith… "PLUS"!

MAKING *It Sure*
(conclusion)
chapter thirteen

FAITH'S BEHAVIOUR REVEALED

The following scriptures have been laid out before you to demonstrate how faith actually behaves itself here in the earth on a daily basis. You will see how faith conducts itself during crises, storms, sicknesses, poverty, wrongful accusations, and many other scenarios. Begin to follow the instructions from Joshua 1:8 and meditate on these scriptures. Build them into your life. Let your faith feed on the living Word of God. Teach and show your faith how it must now conduct itself and behave, for as children of the Most High God there are principles and standards by which we live and now must follow.

Award-winning singer-songwriter Michael W. Smith says:

Reading the Word keeps me in touch with myself. It's the only book I know with a life of its own, and I am most alive when it's working inside me. Few things have had more of an impact on my life than the time I've spent in the Bible.[71]

We have already discovered that faith does not stand alone to accomplish what you read and see in the scriptures. The Apostle John wrote in 1 John 5:4, *"This is the victory that overcometh the world, even our faith."* God designed faith to be victorious.

Roy Talmage Brumbaugh, in his book *The Faith That Wins*, remarks:

> John tells us that the world is made up of three things—'the lust of the flesh,' the lust of the eye,' and thee pride of life.' The world consists of these three things and nothing more. The one victory that overcomes all these things is faith.[72]

Faith, as we have come to know it, does not stand alone in its design and mandate. A team of seven other graces has been commissioned by God to assist faith in its task to grow in the knowledge of Christ. Let your faith then gaze persistently into the mirror of the Word of God so that it may behold itself in the perfect law of liberty.

Bible Teacher Charles Capps says:

> Faith works in the heart (spirit). We need to understand that faith is a spiritual force. It works in the spirit of man. It works in the heart of man… If you get the faith of God in you, it will produce the reality of that thing. But it has to get in the spirit (heart). It won't work in the head.[73]

---

[71] Smith, Michael W. *It's Time to Be Bold* (Nashville, TN: W. Publishing Group, 2003), p. 166.
[72] Brumbaugh, Roy Talmage. *The Faith That Wins* (Chicago, IL: The Bible Institute Colportage Association, 1929), p. 55.
[73] Capps, Charles. *Dynamics of Faith and Confession* (Tulsa, OK: Word of Faith Publishers, 1983), pp. 13–14.

Michael C. Diotte

As you are steadfast and diligent, you will find that your faith grows and rises up in spite of life's storms and circumstances. The way to grow and develop your faith is clear—you must be in the Word of God daily, every day, for the rest of your life. The way to practice and live out your faith is also clear—be grafted into the vine (Jesus) and His vineyard (the family of God). Faith needs to be practiced, and it needs a daily outlet to do so. God's family (Christ's body and His church) is an excellent place to accomplish this, as we are all practicing together to be like Christ.

PRACTICE, PRACTICE, PRACTICE

As we practice our faith together, we can then go on to edify, exhort, and encourage one another (Ephesians 4:16, 4:29, 1 Thessalonians 5:11). As members together in His body, we are each equally responsible to edify (build up) the body of Christ.

Having these three things (exhorting, edifying, encouraging) operating in the family of God (the body of Christ) will ignite everyone's faith into new realms, where God will be able to do far above all that we could ever ask, imagine, or think (Ephesians 3:20).

It is time for the saints of God to align their behaviour to match that of Jesus, our Lord and Saviour. Remember! Faith never focuses on the situation to the point that it is paralyzed. Faith's focus is always on Jesus and the blueprint He left for us to follow—the Word of God.

FAITH KNOWS

Faith knows that the tasks it must accomplish won't always be easy. It knows that Satan and his forces have long been entrenched in this earth, and that it will take diligence, steadfastness, immovableness, and continual abounding in the work of the Lord for it to be successful in rooting out, pulling down, destroying, and throwing down Satan's strongholds (Jeremiah 1:10). Once this is done, the next step of building and planting is activated. Faith knows that doing and accomplishing the commission and work of the Lord is good. 1 Timothy 6:12 says, *"Fight the good fight of faith, lay hold on eternal life, whereunto thou art also called and hast professed a good profession before many witnesses"* (emphasis added). Remember that God is always with you to ensure your success in carrying out His Word. He will work with His Word. He will confirm His Word. He will do His Word as you speak it and operate in it by faith.

SUCCESS

I wish you success as you practice, develop, and operate in the lifestyle and behaviour of faith that God has always had for you. Joshua 10:25 says, *"And Joshua said unto them, Fear not, nor be dismayed, be strong and of good courage: for thus shall the Lord do to all your enemies against whom ye fight."* Once again, welcome to God's realm—the realm of Faith "PLUS."

FAITH *is...*

—The substance of things hoped for, the evidence of things not seen! *"Now faith is the substance of things hoped for, the evidence of things not seen"* (Hebrews 11:1).

—How the just live, not drawing back. *"Now the just shall live by faith: but if any man draw back, my soul shall have no pleasure in him"* (Hebrews 10:38)

—The profession they hold fast to. *"Let us hold fast the profession of our faith without wavering; (for he is faithful that promised)"* (Hebrews 10:23)

—How our heart is fully assured and made true. *"Let us draw near with a true heart in full assurance of faith, having our hearts sprinkled from an evil conscience, and our bodies washed with pure water"* (Hebrews 10:22)

—Coupled with patience and how we inherit the promises of God. *"That ye be not slothful, but followers of them who through faith and patience inherit the promises"* (Hebrews 6:12).

—What we direct toward God. *"Therefore leaving the principles of the doctrine of Christ, let us go on unto perfection; not laying again the foundation of repentance from dead works, and of faith toward God"* (Hebrews 6:1).

—What we mix with the Word of God for our profit. *"For unto us was the gospel preached, as well as unto them: but the word preached did not profit them, not being mixed with faith in them that heard it"* (Hebrews 4:2).

—What we keep during our earthly course until we are finished. *"I have fought a good fight, I have finished my course, I have kept the faith"* (2 Timothy 4:7).

—How we communicate and become effectual by acknowledging every good thing. *"That the communication of thy faith may become effectual by the acknowledging of every good thing which is in you in Christ Jesus"* (Philemon 6).

—An associate of love. *"For in Jesus Christ neither circumcision availeth any thing, nor uncircumcision; but faith which worketh by love"* (Galatians 5:6).

—What we follow after—along with righteousness, love, and peace. *"Flee also youthful lusts: but follow righteousness, faith, charity, peace, with them that call on the Lord out of a pure heart"* (2 Timothy 2:22).

—How we ask. *"But let him ask in faith, nothing wavering. For he that wavereth is like a wave of the sea driven with the wind and tossed"* (James 1:6).

—How we walk. *"Even so faith, if it hath not works, is dead, being alone"* (James 2:17).

—How we obtain a good report. *"And these all, having obtained a good report through faith, received not the promise"* (Hebrews 11:39).

—How we understand by the Word of God. *"Through faith we understand that the worlds were framed by the word of God, so that things which are seen were not made of things which do appear"* (Hebrews 11:3).

—How we pray for others. *"And the prayer of faith shall save the sick, and the Lord shall raise him up; and if he have committed sins, they shall be forgiven him"* (James 5:15).

—How we are kept by God's power. *"Who are kept by the power of God through faith unto salvation ready to be revealed in the last time"* (1 Peter 1:5).

—Placed in God and His Word. *"Who by him do believe in God, that raised him up from the dead, and gave him glory; that your faith and hope might be in God"* (1 Peter 1:21).

Making It Sure

—What we look for in others who we build relationships and serve with. *"Simon Peter, a servant and an apostle of Jesus Christ, to them that have obtained like precious faith with us through the righteousness of God and our Saviour Jesus Christ"* (2 Peter 1:1).

—How we resist the devil. *"Whom resist steadfast in the faith, knowing that the same afflictions are accomplished in your brethren that are in the world"* (1 Peter 5:9).

—The foundation upon which we add, build, and develop our Christian character. *"And beside this, giving all diligence, add to your faith virtue; and to virtue knowledge"* (2 Peter 1:5).

—How we overcome the world and possess our victory. *"For whatsoever is born of God overcometh the world: and this is the victory that overcometh the world, even our faith"* (1 John 5:4).

—What we contend for. *"Beloved, when I gave all diligence to write unto you of the common salvation, it was needful for me to write unto you, and exhort you that ye should earnestly contend for the faith which was once delivered unto the saints"* (Jude 3).

—What we build ourselves upon while praying in the Holy Ghost. *"But ye, beloved, building up yourselves on your most holy faith, praying in the Holy Ghost"* (Jude 20).

—The mystery we hold to in a pure conscience. *"Holding the mystery of the faith in a pure conscience"* (1 Timothy 3:9).

—What we hold fast to with a good conscience. *"Holding faith, and a good conscience; which some having put away concerning faith have made shipwreck"* (1 Timothy 1:19).

—The example we model for others. *"Let no man despise thy youth; but be thou an example of the believers, in word, in conversation, in charity, in spirit, in faith, in purity"* (1 Timothy 4:12).

—What we continue in, being grounded and settled. *"If ye continue in the faith grounded and settled, and be not moved away from the hope of the gospel, which ye have heard, and which was preached to every creature which is under heaven; whereof I Paul am made a minister"* (Colossians 1:23).

—What we are steadfast in, in Christ. *"For though I be absent in the flesh, yet am I with you in the spirit, joying and beholding your order, and the steadfastness of your faith in Christ"* (Colossians 2:5).

Michael C. Diotte

—What we are established in. *"Rooted and built up in him, and stablished in the faith, as ye have been taught, abounding therein with thanksgiving"* (Colossians 2:7).

—How we identify with Christ's death and resurrection. *"Buried with him in baptism, wherein also ye are risen with him through the faith of the operation of God, who hath raised him from the dead"* (Colossians 2:12).

—How we are justified. *"Wherefore the law was our schoolmaster to bring us unto Christ, that we might be justified by faith"* (Galatians 3:24).

—How we become God's children. *"For ye are all the children of God by faith in Christ Jesus"* (Galatians 3:26).

—How we wait in hope of righteousness. *"For we through the Spirit wait for the hope of righteousness by faith"* (Galatians 5:5).

—Part of the fruit of the Spirit in our lives. *"But the fruit of the Spirit is love, joy, peace, longsuffering, gentleness, goodness, faith"* (Galatians 5:22).

—How we are saved by grace. *"For by grace are ye saved through faith; and that not of yourselves: it is the gift of God"* (Ephesians 2:8).

—How Christ dwells in our heart. *"That Christ may dwell in your hearts by faith; that ye, being rooted and grounded in love"* (Ephesians 3:17).

—Doing good, especially to the people of faith, at every opportunity. *"As we have therefore opportunity, let us do good unto all men, especially unto them who are of the household of faith"* (Galatians 6:10).

—Our shield, which protects us from fiery darts. *"Above all, taking the shield of faith, wherewith ye shall be able to quench all the fiery darts of the wicked"* (Ephesians 6:16).

—What abides (dwells and works with) with hope and love. *"And now abideth faith, hope, charity, these three; but the greatest of these is charity"* (1 Corinthians 13:13).

—How we watch and stand, and how strong men and women of God act. *"Watch ye, stand fast in the faith, quit you like men, be strong"* (1 Corinthians 16:13).

—What we strive together with the saints for in the gospel. *"Only let your conversation be as it becometh the gospel of Christ: that whether I come and see you, or else be absent, I may hear of your affairs, that ye stand fast in one spirit, with one mind striving together for the faith of the gospel"* (Philippians 1:27)

—How we walk. *"For we walk by faith, not by sight"* (2 Corinthians 5:7).

—What we abound in. *"Therefore, as ye abound in every thing, in faith, and utterance, and knowledge, and in all diligence, and in your love to us, see that ye abound in this grace also"* (2 Corinthians 8:7).

—What we increase in. *"Not boasting of things without our measure, that is, of other men's labours; but having hope, when your faith is increased, that we shall be enlarged by you according to our rule abundantly"* (2 Corinthians 10:15).

—How we join in Abraham's blessings. *"So then they which be of faith are blessed with faithful Abraham"* (Galatians 3:9).

—Our access road to God. *"By whom also we have access by faith into this grace wherein we stand, and rejoice in hope of the glory of God"* (Romans 5:2).

—How we received the Spirit. *"He therefore that ministereth to you the Spirit, and worketh miracles among you, doeth he it by the works of the law, or by the hearing of faith?"* (Galatians 3:5)

—How the blessings come upon us. *"That the blessing of Abraham might come on the Gentiles through Jesus Christ; that we might receive the promise of the Spirit through faith"* (Galatians 3:14).

—What keeps us from staggering at the promises of God. *"He staggered not at the promise of God through unbelief; but was strong in faith, giving glory to God"* (Romans 4:20).

—How we are justified and have peace with God through Jesus Christ. *"Therefore being justified by faith, we have peace with God through our Lord Jesus Christ"* (Romans 5:1).

—The measure given to every man from God. *"For I say, through the grace given unto me, to every man that is among you, not to think of himself more highly than he ought to think; but to think soberly, according as God hath dealt to every man the measure of faith"* (Romans 12:3).

—The Word we preach from our mouths. *"But what saith it? The word is nigh thee, even in thy mouth, and in thy heart: that is, the word of faith, which we preach"* (Romans 10:8).

—What stands in the power of God. *"That your faith should not stand in the wisdom of men, but in the power of God"* (1 Corinthians 2:5).

—What we are to be full of. *"And Stephen, full of faith and power, did great wonders and miracles among the people... For he was a good man, and full of the Holy Ghost and of faith: and much people was added unto the Lord"* (Acts 6:8; 11:24).

—What we are exhorted to continue in. *"Confirming the souls of the disciples, and exhorting them to continue in the faith, and that we must through much tribulation enter into the kingdom of God"* (Acts 14:22).

—How our hearts are purified. *"And put no difference between us and them, purifying their hearts by faith"* (Acts 15:9).

—How churches are to be established and increase their number. *"And so were the churches established in the faith, and increased in number daily"* (Acts 16:5).

—How we get healed. *"And his name through faith in his name hath made this man strong, whom ye see and know: yea, the faith which is by him hath given him this perfect soundness in the presence of you all... The same heard Paul speak: who steadfastly beholding him, and perceiving that he had faith to be healed... And Jesus said unto him, Go thy way; thy faith hath made thee whole. And immediately he received his sight, and followed Jesus in the way"* (Acts 3:16, 14:9, Mark 10:52).

—What we possess and what is spoken of worldwide. *"First, I thank my God through Jesus Christ for you all, that your faith is spoken of throughout the whole world"* (Romans 1:8).

—The law we are now governed by. *"Where is boasting then? It is excluded. By what law? of works? Nay: but by the law of faith"* (Romans 3:27).

—How righteousness is accounted to us. *"But to him that worketh not, but believeth on him that justifieth the ungodly, his faith is counted for righteousness"* (Romans 4:5).

—To be in His (Jesus') blood. *"Whom God hath set forth to be a propitiation through faith in his blood, to declare his righteousness for the remission of sins that are past, through the forbearance of God"* (Romans 3:25).

—And should be seen. *"And when he saw their faith, he said unto him, Man, thy sins are forgiven thee"* (Luke 5:20).

—What we should be obedient to. *"And the word of God increased; and the number of the disciples multiplied in Jerusalem greatly; and a great company of the priests were obedient to the faith"* (Acts 6:7).

—The realm in which we live and grow from one degree of faith to yet another. *"For therein is the righteousness of God revealed from faith to faith: as it is written, The just shall live by faith"* (Romans 1:17).

This then is the character of faith—the way of faith. This is the conduct of faith and the behaviour of faith. Remember that faith stands not alone, but surrounded, fortified, and encouraged by its alliances and covenant friends, as we discovered in 2 Peter 1:5–7. God has instructed every believer to add to the measure of the faith they received at the new birth and to allow all of the eight graces to work freely in their growth process.

Bestselling author and Bible teacher Chuck Swindoll exhorts us in his book, *So You Want to be Like Christ?*, with these words: "You want to be like Christ? Refuse to surrender to the flesh, surrender instead to the Spirit, and let Him live His life through you.[74]"

This is the God-kind of faith that we have received. It is the language we speak, the dominion in which we walk. It is the land of so much more than ever before. It is the realm of faith… "PLUS."

---

[74] Swindoll, Charles R. *So You Want to Be Like Christ?* (Nashville, TN: W. Publishing Group, 2005), p. 166.